To: Danny ~
   Isn't the Panhandle a
beautiful place! Even though
you're a California guy, your
roots are here + we love you
I hope you'll enjoy the
'romance'.

                  Marilyn McPherson Webb
                       AHS '62

Romancing the Texas Panhandle

AN AFFAIR TO REMEMBER

is published
with the generous support of

CLARENDON ECONOMIC DEVELOPMENT CORPORATION

FIRST NATIONAL BANK OF SPEARMAN–DUMAS

FIRST STATE BANK OF MOBEETIE

WHEELER ECONOMIC DEVELOPMENT CORPORATION

Romancing the

Texas Panhandle

an affair
to remember

MARIWYN McPHERSON WEBB

THE
DONNING COMPANY
PUBLISHERS

The Donning Company Publishers
184 Business Park Drive, Suite 206
Virginia Beach, VA 23462

Steve Mull, General Manager
Barbara B. Buchanan, Office Manager
Richard A. Horwege, Senior Editor
Amanda D. Guilmain, Graphic Designer
Amy Thomann, Imaging Artist
Anne Cordray, Project Research Coordinator
Scott Rule, Director of Marketing
Stephanie Linneman, Marketing Coordinator

Barbara Bolton, Project Director

Library of Congress Cataloging-In-Publication Data
        Webb, Mariwyn McPherson, 1944–
        Romancing the Texas Panhandle : an affair to remember / by Mariwyn McPherson Webb.
        p.   cm.
        Includes index.
        ISBN-13: 978-1-57864-382-0 (hard cover : alk. paper)
        ISBN-10: 1-57864-382-1 (hard cover : alk. paper)
        1. Texas Panhandle (Tex.)—Description and travel. 2. Texas Panhandle (Tex.)—History,
Local. 3. Texas Panhandle (Tex.)—Pictorial works. I. Title.
        F392.P168W43 2006
        917.64'80464—dc22   2006025523
Printed in the USA at Walsworth Publishing Company

Acknowledgments

This book was truly a labor of love for me and for my family. Special thanks to my Mother, Theresa McPherson, who instilled the love of reading and writing in me at a very early age. She also showed me the beauty of the Panhandle, the colorful wildflowers, the interesting wildlife, and the fantastic geological rock formations. Her love of the Panhandle is evident even today in her octogenarian years and she thoroughly enjoyed not only reading the book but giving it a final edit.

Thanks too, to my wonderful husband, Randall Webb, who served as the cartographer, driver, tour guide, grip, photographer, and encourager during the project. I couldn't have done it without him.

Another round of applause goes to my good friend and editor, Pat Hill-Cathcart. Pat has been an integral part of the *romance* of this book and not only served as editor, but also as a research assistant, consultant, photo gatherer, and appointment maker.

Thanks also to Don and Liz Cantrell, publishers and editors of *Accent West Magazine*, for recommending me for the project and for publishing pieces of the book in their monthly magazine.

Last but certainly not least, thanks to my two precious sons, Steffan and Bently Dye. These two special young men encourage, enlighten, and inspire me each day. Just the sound of their voices on the telephone brings a smile to my face and a reason to keep on keeping on.

This book was made possible by generous sponsors and the Panhandle Tourism and Marketing Council. Reference material, historical data, and tourism information came from a variety of sources: Roger Estlack of the *Clarendon Enterprise; Handbook of Texas Online; Wikipedia*, the free encyclopedia; county history books, pamphlets, and brochures provided by individual counties; and in-depth interviews with county historians, economic development committees, and chambers of commerce.

This publication was promoted and marketed by the following Panhandle Area Electric Cooperatives: Rita Blanca Electric, North Plains Electric, Deaf Smith Electric Coop, Greenbelt Electric Coop, Lighthouse Electric Coop, Swisher Electric Coop, Golden Spread Electric Coop, and their support is appreciated.

Contents

Preface

Romancing the Texas Panhandle is truly an appropriate title for this book, for that mysterious, warm, contented feeling comes as one travels through the top twenty-six counties of the Texas Panhandle. The dictionary describes *romance* as "a feeling of excitement and mystery associated with love." That definition fits perfectly with the romance people experience whether living in or traveling around the vast, open prairies. The verb tense means "to court or to woo" and that too happens as the majestic canyons, the limitless plains, and the spectacular sunrises and sunsets first sneak and then snuggle into our hearts.

The Panhandle is certainly a well-kept secret. A part of the Great American Desert, it was once considered useless. When Coronado and his troops came upon the High Plains searching for the fabled cities of gold, they labeled the area a wasteland. Fast forward several hundred years and the same attitude prevailed when the Republic of Texas had little use for the Panhandle, thinking the top of Texas frontier to be very dangerous and fraught with Indian troubles. The Panhandle was the last frontier to be settled when the Red River Wars of 1874–1875 ended the Indian reign. Cheyenne, Kiowa, and Comanche were driven from their lands to reservations, leaving the vast Panhandle open to land-hungry settlers.

Today's Panhandle is full of proud, progressive people who love who they are, what they do, and where they live. The land is vast in that Great American Desert and through the advent of windmills and barbed wire has become a beautiful oasis in Texas. It is often said that if a man wears out a pair of boots in the Panhandle, he will never leave. The area is rich in history and in natural beauty, but it is the people that are its strongest resource. The work ethic is unparalleled, family and faith strong, and community pride abounds.

Pampa's Woody Guthrie penned the now famous song "This Land Is Your Land" and the words can be modified today to read, "This land is your land, this land is my land/From Old Mobeetie to the Caprock Canyons." The ribbon of highway stretches over miles and miles of pancake-flat plains and then drops dramatically into the spectacular Palo Duro, Caprock, and Tulle Canyons. Erosion

has carved spectacular landscapes with colorful cliffs and canyons on the edge of the Caprock. Visitors have the opportunity to experience a close look at geology "in action" and visit a ten-thousand-year-old Native American buffalo kill and butchering site. Palo Duro Canyon is second in size only to the Grand Canyon in Arizona and boasts similar beauty.

Whether you are looking for action and to experience a piece of the cowboys and Indians of the Wild West, or to simply rest and enjoy the quiet, the Panhandle offers it all. It is often said that the beauty, peace, and quiet of the Panhandle makes you feel "a million miles from Monday." Parts of many movies are shot in the Panhandle because of that vast, open prairie and because of the incomparable sunrises and sunsets.

Donley County writer Roger Estlack described it well when he said that the "history has been written by the lives of Indians and explorers, cowmen and plowmen, preachers and teachers, business leaders and laborers and that today this area is the culmination of the dreams of the pioneers who settled here and saw not a formidable wilderness but rather a land of promise."

To experience the Panhandle is truly to experience romance. Try it—for it truly will be an affair to remember.

Armstrong COUNTY

Armstrong County is populated by more than twelve hundred folks who enjoy "country living with a view of city lights." Just twenty miles east of Amarillo sits this bustling rural town of resilient pioneer stock . . . and maybe a "newbie" to the area who has escaped the traffic and bustle of the city for the quiet country life.

When you tell the story of Armstrong County, you are telling the story of the Texas Panhandle. The county's history is colorful and could not be told without many mentions of Colonel Charles Goodnight, who was instrumental in settling the Panhandle.

However, long before Colonel Goodnight's arrival, Francisco Vazquez de Coronado and three hundred soldiers set out from the west coast of Old Mexico and traveled across the Southwest into what is now the Panhandle of Texas. The year was approximately 1541 and many scholars think that Coronado entered from the south and crossed the Palo Duro Canyon on his way to Kansas in search of the fabled "Seven Cities of Gold."

Time passed rather quietly until 1874 when the last battle of the Red River Indian Wars was fought in Palo Duro Canyon. The following year Charles Goodnight drove a herd of cattle into Palo Duro Canyon and started the Home Ranch in what is now the southwestern corner of Armstrong County, becoming the first permanent white settler in the county. A year later, after new roads were built to make travel into area less difficult, Mrs. Goodnight drove a wagonload of supplies into the Canyon and began to make their home.

In 1877 Charles Goodnight and John Adair formed a partnership establishing the famed JA Ranch, making Armstrong County the focal point of the Texas Panhandle. The JA eventually expanded to cover more than one million acres of Panhandle land. Later on, Goodnight moved nearer the railroad and established the Goodnight Buffalo Ranch. The town of Goodnight developed near the ranch headquarters.

Majestic canyons and spectacular color follow the ribbon of Highway 207 on the Plains Trail as it drops off the Caprock down to the Prairie Dog Town Fork of the Red River. Photo by Norbert Schlegel

In the late 1800s settlers began to migrate to the Panhandle to take advantage of the fertile and abundant land. The advent of the windmill and barbed wire made the land productive and attractive to settlers. Around this time approximately fifty "nesters" moved into the Mulberry Flats area five miles east and north of the JA Ranch headquarters and filed for ownership of the land. The JA later traded some plains land to the "nesters" for their land inside the JA so that the JA could fence the entire ranch.

Armstrong County is full of Panhandle "firsts," boasting the first college, the first home for orphans, the first Boy Scout troop west of the Mississippi, and the first County Federated Women's Club of America. The famed and grandiose hotel, The Palace, was the only place to stay overnight between Dallas and Denver in the early 1900s.

Today Armstrong County is a mecca for tourists and history buffs alike. It is steeped in history and so rife with the splendors of nature that even the children traveling through put down their video games to gawk at its majestic canyons. Hunters not only enjoy the breathtaking scenery, but hone their skills each season when deer, sheep, and birds abound.

Opposite page: Cowboy burial site in the famous Goodnight Cemetery in Armstrong County. Photo by William W. Russell

This page: Settlers came to Armstrong County to take advantage of the fertile and abundant land. The advent of the windmill helped make this land useful and productive. Photo by Norbert Schlegel

The drive from Claude south toward Silverton on Highway 207 is one of the most impressive drives in Texas. The beautiful landscape is dotted with crops of wheat and maize. Wheat is the biggest cash crop; Colonel Goodnight is credited for planting wheat in the area. He was known as the Luther Burbank of the Panhandle. The quiet pastoral scene is completed by herds of fattened cattle on the horizon. Suddenly the rural scene plunges into the scenic grandeur of Palo Duro Canyon. A rainbow of colors delights the senses and the nine-mile-wide canyon renders one almost speechless.

The downtown area of Claude, the county seat, is typical of many Texas towns, with a stately classical revival Armstrong County Courthouse built in the middle of the Town Square. The majestic building looms large in the town's epicenter and boasts a courtroom completely restored to as it was in 1915. A favorite watering hole sits just north of the Courthouse and is affectionately known as "the drug store." The original soda fountain still operates, delighting natives and tourists with fountain cherry cokes and the "best darn milkshakes" to be found anywhere.

The Armstrong County Museum is one of the finest in the High Plains. It is a viable complex consisting of a historic museum, a live theater, an attractive art gallery, and a gift shop. The museum's director and volunteers are careful to accept only artifacts that are actually from Armstrong County. The museum presents the history of the events surrounding the settlement of the county—how the cattle industry came to the Texas Panhandle, and the great influence that Colonel Goodnight had the county's development.

The Gem Theater presents live drama and musical performances with its own theater company consisting of local talent. This beautifully restored theater presents

Opposite page: It is not hard to imagine a Kiowa or Comanche riding this horse, in this place, two hundred years ago. Photo by Pat Harkins

This page: Armstrong County is rife with the splendors of nature and so steeped in history that even the children put down their video games to gaze at the beauty. Photo by Darryl Maddox

the Rimstone Revue every third Saturday night under the sponsorship of the Texas Commission on the Arts. Throughout the year the theater schedule includes historic shows about Charles and Mary Ann Goodnight. Panhandle artists display their work in the art gallery next door where Western and Southwestern art is on display throughout the year.

Armstrong County is hailed as the film capital of the Panhandle, with parts of more than ten movies having been shot in the county. One of the first famous Hollywood films to be shot in Claude was the 1963 Paul Newman film, *Hud*. The town was so cooperative with the film's maker that the town's water tower was repainted with the name "Hud." The bank opened at 2:00 in the morning for a particular shot and various citizens enjoyed the being "extras" in the film.

A scene from *Indiana Jones* was shot in the county because of its glorious sunsets. Steve Martin's *A Leap of Faith* was also partially shot in Claude. Television directors often choose Armstrong County for commercials because of the breathtakingly beautiful blue sky, sunrises, sunsets, and frothy white clouds.

The first movie ever to be shot in the county was not a Hollywood blockbuster, but, nonetheless, a priceless historical piece produced in 1916 by none other than Colonel Charles Goodnight. The film was titled *Old Texas* and is still shown from

Opposite page, top left: Petrified wood, egg cavity filled with quartz and woodcuttings preserved. True size of quartz filled cavity is about five mm by two cm. Photo by Darryl Maddox

Opposite page, top right: Only in Claude, Texas, can you find horses watering at the local Dairy Queen. The cowboys are inside having an early morning cup of coffee. Photo by Dick Wilberforce

Opposite page, bottom: Armstrong County's history could not be told without many mentions of Colonel Charles Goodnight, who is pictured here. Photo courtesy of the Panhandle Plains Historical Museum

This page, top left: The stately classical revival Armstrong County Courthouse looms majestically in Claude's epicenter and boasts a courtroom completely restored as it was in 1915. Photo courtesy of the Armstrong County Museum

This page, top right: A typical Texas water tower looms over Claude, Texas, the county seat of Armstrong County. Photo courtesy of the Armstrong County Museum

This page, bottom: African aoudad sheep herd grazing in the Canyon. Photo by Pat Harkins

Opposite page: Another Armstrong County windmill framed by a brilliant Texas sunset. Photo by Darryl Maddox

This page: A myriad of colors radiate in this prehistoric petrified wood. True size is approximately six by five inches. Photo by Darryl Maddox

time to time in the Gem Theater. Colonel Goodnight, who was a longtime friend of Indian Chief Quanah Parker, used his connections with the Indian tribe at Fort Sill, Oklahoma, to bring Indians into Armstrong County for the filming. Goodnight used buffalo from his own prolific herd to portray a reenactment of an early buffalo hunt. The price of admission to see the film was said to be a quarter!

The Charles Goodnight celebration is an annual spring event when the Gem Theater presents live entertainment and tells the story of Colonel Goodnight. Big name stars such as Red Stegal and Pat Gavin and The Buckaroos perform before crowds of adoring country fans.

An annual attraction, the Caprock Roundup, is held the second week of July and will soon be celebrating its seventy-fifth anniversary. The event kicks off with a parade, followed by a rodeo, and always honors the oldest living settlers and the attendees coming from furthest away. (The Chauveaux family from France settled in Armstrong County more than one hundred years ago. Members of that Chauveaux family still farm in the county.) A tasty barbecue is free to all.

A tour of the county would not be complete without a visit to the original Goodnight home, which is currently being restored as a living history ranching center. Another favorite stopping point is the Goodnight Cemetery where Charles and Mary Ann (Molly) Goodnight are buried.

Picturesque, pastoral, pioneers, and *premiers* are just a few of the words that can be used to tell the story of this county full of history and pride.

Briscoe COUNTY

Briscoe County is one of the most scenic, breathtakingly beautiful counties in the Panhandle of Texas. Its terrain is diverse, as part of the county sits on top of the Caprock, while the rest of the county is below it. The magnificent Caprock Canyons and its unexpected Lake Mackenzie make Briscoe County a most desirable tourist destination.

The county rests on the edge of the High Plains along the eastern Caprock escarpment, which separates the Llano Estacado (or Staked Plains) from the Rolling Plains. Briscoe County was organized in 1892, after being separated from the Bexar District in 1876. It was named for Andrew Briscoe, a soldier in the Texas Revolution, who later became a judge and railroad promoter. The county's 887 square miles of irregular terrain range reach thirty-three hundred feet in altitude, dropping to as low as one thousand feet in Tule Canyon.

Geological studies show that pre-Columbian people once lived and worked in what is now Briscoe County. Ruins of irrigation canals and stockades point to a high degree of civilization. The Coronado expedition was one of the area's first recorded visitors. One of Coronado's captains, Maldanado, and his company were hunting buffalo and met a group of Teyas Indians whom they accompanied to their camp. The Teyas camp was apparently situated in a part of Tule Canyon, which is now encompassed by the reservoir.

Soon after, Coronado arrived in the canyon with the remainder of his troops. Among the more valuable results of the encounters between the Spaniards and the Teyas camping in the Tule Canyon at that time are the various recorded descriptions of the people and how they lived. Coronado commented, "They tattoo their bodies and faces, and are large people of very fine appearance. They, too, eat raw meat like the Querechos, live like them, and like them, follow the cattle."

The Plains Apache Indians came next and then were displaced by the Comanche around 1700. The Comanche, who had quickly adopted the horse from the

---

The Ship is a colorful promontory on the Plains Trail on Highway 207 in Briscoe County.
Photo by Norbert Schlegel

Spaniards, began to move into the South Plains from the northwest. Several decades of hostilities between the Comanche and Apache resulted in the Apache's defeat. The Indians found the Canyon recesses rife with buffalo, antelope, and other wild game. Jose Mares and Pedro Vial led trading expeditions through the area in the late 1780s, as did Francisco Amangual in 1808.

The scouts of the Texan Santa Fe Expedition traveled through the Quitaque area in 1841, and in 1852 Captains Randolph B. Marcy and George B. McClellan followed the Prairie Dog Town Fork of the Red River through the area of the present county. The area became a favorite stopping point of the Comanchero traders because the breaks west of Quitaque contained abundant springs.

White captives of Comanche raiders were often separated and traded to other Indian bands or Comancheros in the notorious Valley of Tears. That ended after Colonel Ranald S. Mackenzie's Fourth United States Calvary crisscrossed the county in pursuit of the "Mongols of the West" in 1872, and again after they battled the Indians at Tule Creek in 1874. On September 29, 1874, after their crucial victory at Palo Duro Canyon the day before, Mackenzie's troops slaughtered more than one thousand Indian horses at Tule Canon.

The battle was a catastrophe for the Indians; the Comanche stronghold was broken and Briscoe County was now open for settlement by the impatient whites. Open-range cattleraising came into the area and the Quitaque "Lazy F" Ranch was established in 1878. This ranch was added to the JA Ranch properties in 1882, fenced the following year, and was a primary influence on the county's early

Beautiful Lake Mackenzie is popular with water enthusiasts throughout the area. It is located twelve miles northwest of Silverton and twenty-seven miles east of Tulia. Photo by Emmett E. Tomlin

economy. By 1890 a few stock farmers and small ranchers had begun settling on the periphery lands of the "Lazy F."

The town of Quitaque sprouted in 1890 as a stage stop, and merchants and other businessmen soon arrived. The town of Silverton was platted in 1891, and organization of the county began. Soon a petition was circulated, the electorate officially organized, and Silverton was chosen as the county seat.

By 1900 the population of Briscoe County had grown exponentially; school districts had been established and immigrant farmers had introduced various crops to the region, primarily wheat, sorghum, and cotton. Cotton was first grown in Briscoe County on an experimental basis, but became one of the county's most important crops by 1930.

During this time ranches gave way to farms, until most of the arable lands were under cultivation. This agricultural growth brought a railroad to the county. Before the 1920s all freight came in wagons, then later in automobiles from Amarillo or Estelline. In 1925 the Fort Worth and Denver Railway built into the region; a branch line was completed from Estelline westward to Quitaque and Silverton.

The county's agricultural economy suffered during the Great Depression and the number of farms decreased dramatically. Cotton production fell by more than 30 percent.

Mule deer pose for the camera at Briscoe County's Lake Mackenzie. Abundant wildlife includes mule deer, aoudad sheep, coon, badger, possum, porcupine, wild turkey, quail, pheasant, duck, geese, and bald eagle. Photo by Emmett E. Tomlin

Today Briscoe County continues to rely heavily on agriculture as a major source of revenue. Cotton, grains sorghums, wheat, vegetables, and melons are some of the crops grown on the county's more than forty thousand irrigated acres.

Silverton, the county seat, was aptly named because of the silvery reflections of the shallow lakes in the area. The Briscoe County Courthouse was erected in 1893, and the following year a jail built of stone from Tule Canyon was completed. The jail's first occupant was the county sheriff who was jailed as a joke during the opening ceremony. The Briscoe County Historical Society operates a small museum in the County Courthouse basement. The Old Jail Museum is a popular tourist destination. This old stone jailhouse is the oldest building in the county and features an old jail office with cells upstairs. It is located on the Courthouse Square and features a restored windmill outside.

Silverton has suffered from prairie fires, grasshoppers, dust storms, and cyclones. Its worst disaster occurred in 1957 when a tornado killed twenty-one people and did more than a million dollars in damage. The dedicated citizens quickly rebuilt and Silverton is now a commercial center for a large and productive farming and ranching area that includes spectacular scenery in Palo Duro Canyon, Tule Canyon, and the edge of the Caprock. A small airfield is located east of town, and the Haynes Boy Scout Camp is in the canyon breaks eight miles to the east. Silverton is on the Ozark Trail and on the Texas Plains Trail.

Vivid illustrations of High Plains topography come into view along Texas Highways 86 and 286 North. Travelers can see the immense proportions of High Plains agricultural areas, where the land is typically flat. Then quickly, in startling contrast, they can view the effect of erosion where watercourses have carved plunging, colorful canyons.

The first settler in Silverton's neighboring community of Quitaque was the Comanchero trader Jose Piedad Tafoya, who operated a trading post, trading

dry goods and ammunition to the Comanches in exchange for rustled livestock. In 1877 George Baker drove a herd of about two thousand cattle to the Quitaque area, where he headquartered the "Lazy F" Ranch. Charles Goodnight later bought the "Lazy F" and introduced the name *Quitaque*, which he believed was the Indian word for "end of the trail." Another legend has it that the name *Quitaque* was derived from two buttes in the area that resembled piles of horse manure, the real meaning of the Indian word! Another story is that the name was taken from the Quitaca Indians, whose name was translated by white settlers as "whatever one steals." Whatever the origin of the name, all can agree that *Quitique* (pronounced Kit-a-Kway) is definitely difficult to spell.

The small picturesque town has two city parks, a community center, and a fire station. Numerous Russian pines have been planted throughout the town as a part of a state beautification program. Hunters are drawn to the area because of its beauty, rugged terrain, and abundant wildlife. Guided hunts are available, as are some cabin rentals. Some of the largest mule deer in Texas are seen in the area, as well as wild hog, sand hill crane, pheasant, quail, dove, and waterfowl.

Caprock Canyons State Park and Trailway make Quitaque a favorite visitor's destination. The beautiful and rugged park covers 13,960 acres of one of the state's most scenic regions. Erosion has carved spectacular landscapes at the edge of the Caprock. Colorful cliffs and canyons, abundant wildlife, including African aoudad sheep, mule deer, and golden eagles abound. Park visitors enjoy sightseeing, hiking trails, picnicking, fishing, swimming, and boating in the one-hundred-acre Lake Theo. They also have the opportunity to experience a close look at geology "in action" and visit a ten-thousand-year-old Native American buffalo kill and butchering site.

Today the state's largest bison herd lives in the park. These fifty-three magnificent animals are in an enclosed 320 acres, and an observation platform makes them easy to see. This is the only DNA pure southern bison herd in the world.

Caprock Canyons State Park, opened in 1982, is situated one hundred miles southeast of Amarillo, and offers something for everyone: boating, camping, hiking, horseback riding, mountain biking, fishing, lake swimming, a scenic drive, guided tours, and seasonal concessions with horse rentals. Almost ninety miles of multiuse trails range from the easily traversed to the very difficult "in-offs," with steep climbs and descents that are recommended only for the experienced equestrian and mountain bike riders. The recently completed audio driving guide to the park is like having a tour guide on your own schedule—and it's free!

The park harbors numerous species of wildlife such as African aoudad sheep, mule and white-tailed deer, raccoon, coyote, bobcat, opossum, porcupine, fox, and more than 175 species of birds. The pride of Caprock Canyons is, of course, the large buffalo herd and the rarely seen golden eagle. Lake Theo offers great fishing opportunities, featuring bass, catfish, and crappie.

Caprock Canyons Trailway runs more than sixty-four miles through Briscoe, Floyd, and Hall Counties. It moves through the cultivated fields of the Texas High Plains, drops into the rugged canyons of the Caprock escarpment, and winds down into the famous Red River Valley. A unique feature along the trail near the escarpment is a thousand-foot abandoned railroad tunnel, which is on the National Register of Historic Places as one of only a few such tunnels in Texas.

Beautiful Lake Mackenzie is popular with water enthusiasts throughout the area. It is located twelve miles northwest of Silverton and twenty-seven miles east of Tulia. The 45,500-acre lake features boat ramps with floating docks, thirty-eight RV hookups, a playground, and picnic tables with outdoor grills, a large shelter, nature trail, and all-terrain vehicle (ATV) trails. All types of watercraft are allowed on the lake, including powerboats, jet skis, and sailboats.

Abundant wildlife at Lake Mackenzie includes mule deer, aoudad sheep, coon, badger, possum, porcupine, wild turkey, quail, pheasant, duck, geese, and bald eagle. The lake is stocked with several species of catfish, crappie, bass, striper, walleye, and perch. The lake is a popular destination for riders of ATV, four-wheelers, and dirt bikes.

Spectacularly beautiful Briscoe County is a "must see" in the Texas Panhandle. It is the place where geology and ancient history come to life.

Carson  COUNTY

Carson County is comprised of the charming rural communities of Panhandle, White Deer, and Groom. The county is reminiscent of 1960s television comedies such as *Father Knows Best* and *Leave It to Beaver*. The center of community life in these Carson County towns is the schools, and school spirit is alive and well in residents from eight to eighty. Pride in the schools is apparent whether the topic is academic excellence, the program for challenged students, or the successful sports teams. Many athletic playoff events are held in the communities, bringing an influx of visitors and cash each year. The town of Panhandle is not only the county seat, but also the center for education, providing an extraordinary academic background for its residents, allowing them to compete with graduates from much more cosmopolitan areas.

While some High Plains communities tout that "cotton is king," Panhandle boasts that "education is king." Ninety percent of Panhandle's ranchers and farmers hold bachelor's degrees; more than one hundred hold master's degrees. This is an unusually high number, representing more degrees in agriculturally related studies than in any of the other Panhandle counties. Education is most definitely of paramount importance to the community.

The county has always been favorable to business and businessmen, as exemplified by the story of local entrepreneur, Marvin Sparks. Sparks had polio as a child and as an adult he wanted to find a way to help others with this affliction. He began looking at whirlpools and athletic equipment and now owns a multimillion-dollar corporation, Vibrawhirl, which is the fourth-largest company supplying artificial turf for running tracks and baseball stadiums in the country. His company is still located in the town of Panhandle and employs more than two hundred people. Another entrepreneurial Panhandle man created TCBY, the famed yogurt brand.

Carson County's population is sixty-five hundred and growing. Panhandle, its largest town is the only town in the Texas Panhandle that has grown in population

The full moon illuminates Interstate 40 for the lone trucker. A part of old Route 66 is seen in the foreground. Photo by Norbert Schlegel

every year for the last twelve years. As many small communities are decreasing in size, Panhandle is actually growing. Its close proximity to Amarillo and, more importantly, to the Pantex Ordnance Plant, offers many Panhandle residents the opportunity to enjoy small town living while working in nearby Amarillo.

Carson County has the second-largest average weekly individual income in Texas. Education is again the primary reason, because a majority of Carson County residents are college educated and many work as engineers and technicians at the Pantex, Celenese, and Conoco-Phillips plants. Panhandle is the hub of the "Magic Circle," in the center of activity around Amarillo, Pampa, and Borger.

Perhaps in part because of the education and income levels of its residents, the town of Panhandle is extremely well maintained. The newly refurbished Main Street boasts brick streets laid by the WPA in the 1930s, and renovated streetlights. The lights are copies of the actual streetlights of the early 1920s. Planters and trees add to the downtown area's ambiance. This bustling burg of twenty-six hundred is home to two banks, eleven churches, a fine museum, and a country club with a nine-hole golf course open to the public.

The Square House Museum on State Highway 207 is considered one of the nation's finest small museums, attracting more than twenty-five thousand visitors each year. It is the major tourist attraction in the county, has appeared in the *Michelin Tour Guide,* and is often featured in travel magazines. It was the third museum in Texas, and the seventeenth in the entire country, to be accredited. The museum is unique because while other museums focus on the history of the community and local artifacts, the Square House Museum more broadly focuses on the State of Texas and on the nation. The center of the museum's facilities is the 1887 Square House, a small wooden frame residence with a rooftop widows' walk. The museum

The Square House Museum on State Highway 207 is considered one of the nation's finest small museums.
Photo by Viola Moore

complex features pioneer implements, a Santa Fe Railway caboose, a half dugout, and a memorial exhibition dedicated to man's quest for freedom. Fine art by artists from across the United States is displayed on a rotating basis and then stored in the museum's state-of-the-art climate-controlled storage area. This exceptional museum is a High Plains "must see," displaying in excess of thirty-five thousnd artifacts.

The sister cities of White Deer, Groom, and Skelleytown are home to the remainder of Carson County's population base. The primary growth of these towns is due to the discovery of oil and gas in Carson County in 1919.

White Deer is named for nearby White Deer Creek, where, according to local legend, an Indian saw an albino deer drinking from the creek. White Deer is on the Ozark Trail and each Christmas participates in the Festival of the Trail Tour. This Polish community remains true to its roots and holds an annual Polish sausage fest each year. The town recently received an important designation from the Texas Historical Commission as an Outstanding Rural Community.

Tourists are fascinated with the Llano Estacado Wind Farm located in White Deer. There are two sets of ninety-six wind generators on a ridge just outside of town. These wind generators harness the ever-abundant Panhandle wind and convert it to electricity. It's an amazing sight to see as you drive through the county and notice the oil pump jacks dotted along the horizon; then, just a blink away, the wind farm with the blades turning, harnessing the power of wind.

Groom, just a few miles away, was a notorious town in the 1920s. Its reputation was earned not because of famous gun battles or houses of ill repute, but because of the much-talked-about Jericho Gap. This muddy road was the bane of hundreds of cars every time it rained. The black gumbo soil served to bog down even the lightest vehicle. Tourists were continually worried about when they would come upon the terrible Jericho Gap. The economy of Groom prospered because stranded visitors were often forced to say in town as they waited for wreckers to come and free their cars.

Two sets of ninety-six wind generators on a ridge just outside of town harness the abundant Panhandle wind and convert it to electricity. Photo by Dale Moore

Wind is harnessed by the old and the new. Photo by Randall Webb

Today travelers look forward to stopping in Groom at the site a major tourist attraction. Truckers, cyclists, and automobiles traveling on Interstate 40 stop to see the second-largest cross in the Western Hemisphere. This majestic cross is 190 feet tall and can't be missed from Interstate 40. There are also near life-sized bronze statues representing the Stations of the Cross around the foot of the giant metal cross. On a hill just west of the cross is a crucifix scene, and east of the cross is a memorial. The area is enhanced by a climate-controlled building housing information about the Shroud of Turin. Many truckers use the site to hold private services on Sunday mornings. There is a highway rest stop nearby.

Carson County sits squarely in the center of the Texas Panhandle on the eastern edge of the High Plains. Like other Panhandle counties, it is nine hundred square miles of level to rolling prairie land, with dark clay and loamy soil that make the county productive for farming.

The history of the county is not unlike that of other Texas Panhandle counties, with prehistoric hunters first occupying the area and then the Indians' arrival. American buffalo hunters penetrated the Panhandle in the early 1870s as they slaughtered the great southern herd. The ensuing Indian Wars, culminated by the Red River War of 1874, led to the extermination of the buffalo and the removal of the Comanche to Indian Territory. The Panhandle was now opened to settlement, and Carson County was established in 1876 when its territory was marked off from the Bexar District.

As in other counties, the railroad played a major part in Carson County's development. Some early settlers earned money hauling bones of slaughtered buffalo to the railroad to be shipped east to fertilizer plants, while others farmed, ranched, or set up retail establishments. A sanatorium and several doctors' offices made Panhandle a haven for health seekers. The local hotel hosted Buffalo Bill Cody and other distinguished guests. The town had a thriving ice and coal business and grain

Groom is host to the second-largest cross in the Western Hemisphere. The majestic cross is 190 feet tall. Photo by Darryl Maddox

elevators rose along the tracks. At times as many as sixty-five thousand cattle were held in the loading pens awaiting railroad shipment.

The famed JA Ranch of Charles Goodnight and John G. Adair and the Turkey Track Ranch both grazed large ranges in Carson County by 1880.

Water had to be brought to the town of Panhandle by railroad from the area of Miami in Roberts County, and then carried in barrels on wagons to homesteads. This was a challenge to the community until it was found that abundant underground water could be pumped to the surface by windmills. That discovery, together with the selling of White Deer lands to ranchers and farmers in 1902, greatly increased the area's attractiveness.

By 1920 the county was well established and ready for the oil boom that hit the area. By 1930, Panhandle had become the center of a large natural gas field and Carson County had a diversified economy now based on ranching, farming, petroleum, and transportation.

Today Carson County is a growing and desirable place to live and work, with a stable economy still based on ranching, farming, oil, transportation, and the Pantex Ordnance Plant.

Opposite page, left: Strong Panhandle winds help to create a fiercely dynamic sunrise. Photo by Norbert Schlegel

Opposite page, right: Not only do sunflowers light up the fields and pastures, they have also become an important cash crop. Photo by Norbert Schlegel

This page, top left: The Panhandle Inn hosts weary travelers. The inn's design is similar to that of the Governor's Palace in Santa Fe, New Mexico. Photo by Roy Lane

This page, top right: The old railroad depot was built in 1927. It is both historic and useful, as it now houses the City Hall. Photo by Roy Lane

*This page, bottom: Yucca and a barbed wire fence. The Spaniards derived **Llano Estacado** from the word **yucca**, meaning "Staked Plains."* Photo by Roy Lane

Castro  COUNTY

Dimmitt, the county seat of Castro County is steeped in history, some long past and some more recent. The town was established in 1891, slightly later other Panhandle towns began. As people started to populate the county, the Bedford Town and Land Company purchased land as near the center of the county as possible for the purpose of establishing the county seat.

H. G. Bedford, president of the company, was appointed the agent and given a power of attorney to sell lots in the town site named Dimmitt. The name was selected to honor Reverend W. C. Dimmitt, who was Bedford's Civil War friend, a member of the Bedford Town and Land Company, and a circuit-riding preacher. Soon a hotel was built, a well was drilled for water, and the newly formed town of Dimmitt was on its way to prosperity.

Dimmitt was selected as the county seat over its sister town, Castro City. Hard feelings over the selection led to the famous gunfight between Ira Aten, a retired Texas Ranger, and Andrew McClelland. The story goes that Mr. Aten had retired from the Texas Rangers because his love interest, Miss Imogen Boyce, refused to marry a lawman. Her cousin suggested that Ira homestead land in Castro County near the XIT Ranch as an investment for the future. Aten bought 160 acres just east of the proposed town site of Dimmitt in 1890 and began to make improvements by digging a dugout.

Other settlers moved into the county and politicking began as to whether the county seat should be in Dimmitt or Castro City. Andrew and Hugh McClelland, brothers from Tennessee who had settled just east of Plainview in 1887, came over to Castro County to help organize the county and establish the Dimmitt town site as the county seat. Andrew was an attorney, and both he and Hugh were reputed to be fast and able with the guns they wore.

In an open meeting, the McClellands presented the advantages of the Dimmitt town site, then Ira Aten stood to discuss the advantages of the Castro City town site.

One of Castro County's spectacular sunsets highlights a bodark (Osage orange) fence post that has been standing for more than one hundred years. Photo by Norbert Schlegel

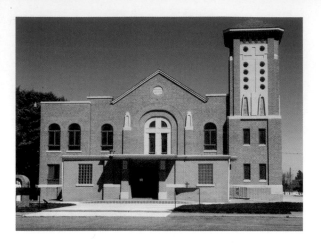

Andrew McClelland stood up and called Aten a liar! Those were fighting words, but Aten said that his Ranger training prohibited him from using a gun where women and children were present. He would, however, be happy to settle the matter with McClelland at another time. Dimmitt was ultimately chosen as the county seat, which was okay with Aten, because it was for the general good of the county.

A few days later, Ira Aten strapped on his Ranger pistol and rode into town to settle the matter with McClelland. The "shootout on Jones Street" occurred in front of the general store. Aten asked McClelland if he still thought Aten was a liar. McCleland replied in the affirmative but said that he was unarmed. Aten told McClelland to go get his gun and, in just a few minutes, McClelland came out of the store with a pistol in each hand, firing as he moved up the street toward Aten. Bullets flew and the shootout was soon over. Aten wounded Andrew McClelland and his brother Hugh, but was later acquitted of assault charges. A short time later he was appointed Castro County sheriff. Downtown Dimmitt boasts a historical marker to the "shootout on Jones Street" and the actual gun Aten used is on display in the Castro County Museum.

Another, more recent piece of county history occurred in the early 1940s when a prisoner of war camp was located in Castro and Deaf Smith Counties. The campsite, three and a half miles southeast of Hereford, was more than eight hundred acres in size and housed mainly Italian prisoners. It was called "The Criminal Camp" because it housed the Italians who refused to go back to Italy and fight for the Americans. Many of them were doctors, lawyers, and other professional men, and most were older in age. More than five thousand prisoners and 750 United States military personnel lived at the camp in the three and a half years that it existed. The county is proud that only five of the prisoners died during their internment in Castro County. A number of prisoners who were skilled craftsmen and glassworkers constructed a chapel in honor of their five comrades who died in the camp. They were buried on each side of the chapel. After the war, their bodies were exhumed and returned to Italy.

The Italians were hard workers and added value to the nearby communities.

SHOOT-OUT ON JONES STREET

AT AN 1891 MEETING TO DISCUSS THE SELECTION OF A CASTRO COUNTY SEAT, WORDS WERE EXCHANGED BETWEEN IRA ATEN, A RETIRED TEXAS RANGER SPEAKING ON BEHALF OF CASTRO CITY, AND ANDREW McCLELLAND, A SPOKESMAN FOR DIMMITT. THE INFLAMMATORY REMARKS LED TO A GUNFIGHT BETWEEN THE TWO MEN ON DEC. 23, FIVE DAYS AFTER DIMMITT WAS CHOSEN COUNTY SEAT. IN AN EXCHANGE OF SHOTS IN THE MIDDLE OF JONES STREET, ATEN WOUNDED ANDREW McCLELLAND AND HIS BROTHER HUGH. ATEN WAS ACQUITTED OF THE ASSAULT CHARGES AND A SHORT TIME LATER WAS APPOINTED CASTRO COUNTY SHERIFF.

(1983)

Left: The Holy Family Catholic Church of Nazareth stands proudly in the downtown area. The first Catholic parish was established in 1902 and the church remains a focal point of community activities today. Photo by Randall Webb

Right: This present Castro County Courthouse was built out of sandstone in the 1940s. It is the third County Courthouse; the first was built in 1892, and another in 1906. Photo by Randall Webb

Bottom: This historical marker tells the tale of the shoot-out on Jones Street between a retired Texas Ranger and a spokesperson for Dimmitt. Photo by Randall Webb

Some were sent to Dumas to work at the American Zinc Company, while others worked in the fields gathering crops. A few of them were fine artists and are responsible for the beautiful murals, stained glass, and woodcarvings at Saint Mary's Catholic Church in Umbarger.

Today Dimmitt is home to four thousand people. The center of its economy is agriculture. The area excels in producing large yields of corn, cotton, wheat, sunflowers, sugar beets, and vegetables. Cattle feeding operations and dairies round out the county's economy; Castro County is the second-largest cattle feeding area in the state. Dairies are prominent in the county, with herds totaling more than fifty thousand dairy cows within a forty-five mile radius.

But agriculture isn't all that Castro County offers. The county boasts a museum housed in The Old Carter House, circa 1908. It features county photos, artifacts, early farm equipment, and a furnished half-dugout.

Quilters from all over the country flock into Dimmitt the first weekend in April to enjoy and participate in the Ogallala Quilt Festival. Intricately designed quilts are on display during the annual competition.

Another unusual county event is the annual citywide garage sale held the first week of June. Its eighteen-year history draws people from area towns to this giant sale. The Chamber of Commerce distributes a location map at eight in the morning and the bargain hunt begins. Food vendors are gathered around the Square and a festive atmosphere prevails.

Although Dimmitt may not have grown in population recently, the town is still very much alive and well and is known as the town full of "cattle, commerce, crops, and cowboys."

Childress COUNTY

One hundred sixteen miles southeast of Amarillo and 108 miles northwest of Wichita Falls a thriving, bustling town appears on the horizon. More than seven thousand people live and work in Childress, Texas, county seat of Childress County. Although ranching and farming are the mainstay of the county's economic base, with more than two hundred growing days a year, a Texas State Prison adds more than four hundred jobs and even more dollars to the community. Agricultural income is earned primarily from cotton, wheat, hay, grain sorghums, peanuts, cattle, and Angora goats.

The park system in Childress is unparalleled in the state, with more than ninety acres of parks. Fair Park Lake is available for community use and stocked with fish. The lake is surrounded by acres of park with five timber bridges, a walking trail, RV hookups, barbecue grills, a swimming pool, designated campsites, tennis courts, baseball fields, softball fields, and a rodeo arena. A beautiful eighteen-hole municipal golf course completes the recreation complex.

Many athletic contests are held in Childress because of its incredible facilities. The Childress High School's gymnasium comfortably accommodates fourteen hundred people with state-of-the art stadium seating and hosts several tournaments throughout the year.

The Greenbelt Bowl Football Classic is genuinely a "classic" in the area, having been held annually for more that fifty-six years. Both area and regional high school seniors are nominated by their coaches to play in this exciting clash of helmets.

Fair Park is used for countless events throughout the year and is a beacon of fun and recreation for area residents and tourists. Christmas in the Park has become a widely touted annual event when the whole park comes alive with Christmas lights and displays. The main footbridge is a romantic twinkling fairyland and the animated, lighted displays delight young and old alike. Christmas in the Park lights

The majestic Childress County Courthouse, flanked by miles and miles of red brick streets, is in itself a wonder. Photo by Randall Webb

up from Thanksgiving until New Year's Day. The synergy of the town is apparent in this huge undertaking.

The Red River Gun and Knife Show, along with its sanctioned chili cook-off, is an annual September event. It is held in the City Auditorium, which is housed in Fair Park.

Autumn also brings bikers to the county for the "Tour de Cotton Bike Run" which begins in Fair Park with different routes heading into the countryside. Hundreds of bikers look forward to this annual event where the most seasoned biker can compete in the 50k run and the faint of heart can still enjoy participating in a 5k or 10k run.

Like most Panhandle towns, Childress is on the rodeo circuit and is proud to be the home of rodeo legends Strand Smith, Roy Cooper, and Freddie Cordell. The Old Settlers Rodeo comes to life in mid-July each year and with it comes the all-school reunion.

Nearby Baylor and Childress Lakes provide excellent fishing and camping in the area. Plenty of campsites and RV hookups are available. Fishermen from all over the

This page, left: The park system in Childress is unparalleled in the state, with more than ninety acres of parks. The swimming pool is a popular watering hole during the hot, dry summers. Photo courtesy of the Childress Chamber of Commerce

This page, middle: Fair Park Bridge is a popular attraction in Childress County. It becomes a romantic twinkling fairyland at Christmas time. Photo courtesy of the Childress Chamber of Commerce

This page, right: A nostalgic brick walkway leads to this gazebo in Fair Park. Photo courtesy of the Childress Chamber of Commerce

Opposite page: Cotton is a mainstay of the county's economy. Other agricultural income comes from wheat, hay, grain sorghums, peanuts, cattle, and Angora goats. Photo courtesy of the Childress Chamber of Commerce

country enjoy exceptional bass fishing and bass tournaments throughout the year. Both lakes are well known for their fine "lunkers." Baylor Lake is just nine miles northwest of Childress and has more than forty-one thousand feet of shoreline. Just across from Baylor Lake lies Childress Lake with more than twelve thousand feet of shoreline. Both lakes are available for public use.

A drive through downtown Childress is like taking a step into the past. Stately old buildings with architecture dating back to the 1920s still stand proudly. Some have been refurbished while some remain tall but sadly deserted. The majestic Childress County Courthouse, flanked by miles and miles of red brick streets, is itself a wonder. The grand old Palace Theater is being refurbished by the Childress Theater Company and will be used as a dinner theater and for community activities.

The Palace Theater in its glory days was home to many traveling entertainers, one of which was the legendary cowboy Gene Autry. In 1938, Autry, just a little down on his luck, rode into the small railroad town of Childress. He asked the theater manager if there was any work to be had. The enterprising manager seized the opportunity and offered the cowboy one hundred dollars—a lot of money during the Depression era. For one hundred dollars this cowboy wouldn't be taking tickets or sweeping up popcorn. He would be pickin' and a singin' and entertaining the adoring crowds. Legend has it that Autry's horse, Champion, also made an appearance on stage that night!

Also of note on display in the downtown area is a shiny black railroad engine. Engine No. 501 was a gift to the city from the Fort Worth and Denver Railway and has delighted children and railroad buffs for years. The engine is an important part of the county's history because Childress' livelihood once centered on the railroad that ultimately created the town in 1887.

Romancing the Texas Panhandle

Opposite page: Engine No. 501, was a gift to the city of Childress from the Fort Worth and Denver Railway and has delighted children and railroad buffs for years. Photo by Randall Webb

This page, top: Baylor Lake provides excellent fishing and camping in the area. Photo courtesy of the Childress Chamber of Commerce

This page, bottom: This beautiful white tail buck is typical of those that roam the prairies and ranches of Childress County. Photo courtesy of the Childress Chamber of Commerce

Childress County is touted as and truly is "The Gateway to the Panhandle." It was established in 1887 and derived its name from George C. Childress, the author of the Texas Declaration of Independence. In 1887 the county's population was three hundred and consisted of two communities just four miles apart. The towns' names were Childress and Henry.

An election was held to determine the location for the county seat, but questions concerning the legality of voting procedures caused the election to be nullified. Before another election could be scheduled, the town fathers made a compromise. The agreement was that the citizens of Childress would move to Henry and the name Henry would be no more. The town would be named Childress City and would become the seat of government.

Going back in time even further, Childress County was a great pasture land of huge herds of buffalo and wild horses and was considered a part of the "Wild Wild West." During the Civil War, military outposts were located at Illinois Bend and Red River Station in Montague County, and at Fort Belknap near Albany, Texas. Everything west of that line was designated as the "Wild West."

The railroad played a significant role in the development of the county. In 1887, the year the Childress County was formed, the Fort Worth and Denver Railway extended its transportation rail service and shipping lines through Childress and in 1901 a fire at the Clarendon Round House changed the course of history. The enterprising citizens of Childress set out to make Childress the railway's division headquarters for the train crews. After months of planning, contracts, and proposals, the Fort Worth and Denver made Childress the division headquarters.

The railroad is credited for the rapid growth in Childress, which by 1913 was home to more than thirteen thousand people. Many of those townsfolk were working at the Fort Worth and Denver Railway. Burlington Northern Lines soon took over the Fort Worth and Denver, establishing its area warehouses and maintenance station in Childress.

The railway's headquarters move from Clarendon to Childress brought a railroad family named Chrysler to the area. Mr. Chrysler was a railroad engineer whose son, Walter P. Chrysler, made a decision to move his automobile shop to Childress. Yes, Walter P. Chrysler was the founder of Chrysler Motor Corporation and, although the Chryslers didn't live in Childress long, the very famous personage of Mr. Chrysler lingers on.

Cotton and cattle continue to be the mainstays of commerce in the growing community of Childress. Rugged ranch land borders the Red River to the town's north and the natural canyons to its south.

Collingsworth

COUNTY

Collingsworth County sits on the eastern edge of the Texas Panhandle, bordered on the east by Oklahoma. The county's 894 square miles of river breaks and rolling prairie are both beautiful and stark, depending upon the season. Just about half of the terrain is suitable for farming, producing cotton, peanuts, wheat, and grain sorghums. Ranching remains a strong influence on the economy of the county. A small amount of oil and gas production is also notable.

Apache Indians were the primary occupants of the area until about 1700, when Kiowa and Comanche arrived. These strong Indian tribes dominated the Panhandle until the United States Army defeated them in the Red River War of 1874. The tribes were then removed permanently to reservations in the Indian Territory of Oklahoma.

The Texas legislature formed Collingsworth County from land that had been previously a part of Bexar and Young Counties. As in other parts of the Panhandle, buffalo hunters roamed the county, slaughtering thousands from the great herds and thus opening the frontier for cattlemen.

By the late 1870s, ranchers came into Collingsworth County. The Rowe Brothers Ranch established its large holdings in southwestern Collingsworth County. By 1880 the United States census reported six people (three white and three black) living in the county.

Other large ranches were established in the early 1880s and controlled most of the county's land. William and James Curtis claimed the southeastern part of the county for their Diamond Trail Ranch in 1880. In 1883 the Rocking Chair Ranch, an English venture like that of the Rowe brothers, bought alternate sections of most of the remaining land in the northeastern part of the county, enabling them to control twice as much land as they actually owned.

A severe drought in 1884–87 and an even more destructive blizzard in 1886 ruined many of the ranchers and some changes in Texas land laws made it more difficult for them to control the state lands desired by settlers. The large ranches

Who needs the Caribbean? Just look at the exquisite spectrum of colors on the Salt Fork of the Red River. Photo by Norbert Schlegel

began to split into smaller spreads, established by new settlers. Some of these new settlers began farming in the county.

Wellington became the county seat and in 1891 the new city was platted and the construction of the Collingsworth County Courthouse began. Wellington was named after the Duke of Wellington by one of the English owners of the Rocking Chair Ranch. A relative of the Earl of Aberdeen, one of the Rocking Chair's owners, had been with the Duke at Waterloo; thus the name Wellington. The county seat was decided between Pearl City and Wellington by a hotly contested election, with the ranchers promoting Wellington. The voters were offered five town lots each if they would choose Wellington for the county seat.

Wellington began to grow and expand after 1900 and cotton began to rival cattle economically. In 1910 the Wichita Falls and Wellington Railway Company of Texas built a line from the Oklahoma-Texas border to Wellington and helped to tie the area to national markets and encourage development.

The Dust Bowl and Great Depression of the Dirty Thirties interrupted Collingsworth County's expansion and the population began to decrease; however the remaining citizens moved ahead and in 1931 built a larger County Courthouse, as the Fort Worth and Denver Northern Railway reached the town. By 1934 Wellington had paved streets, natural gas, and a sewage system. A compress, several gins, four churches, a hospital, and many other businesses filled the town.

Today Wellington remains a farming and ranching center, with several working gins and grain elevators. The town's weekly newspaper, The *Wellington Leader,* has

Opposite page, left: Wellington
began to grow and expand after
1900 and cotton began to rival
cattle economically. The economy
is now based almost totally on
cotton and peanuts. Shown here is
a cotton stripper at work. Photo by
Becky Asher

Opposite page, right: Art
Deco detailing on the 1932
Collingsworth County Courthouse
in Wellington. Photo by Wes Reeves

This page: The Bonnie and Clyde
escapade has been told and retold
throughout the years and has made
Wellington a place to visit for
those interested in these notorious
criminals. This historical marker
is on U.S. Highway 83 north of
Wellington. Photo by Norbert Schlegel

been owned and operated by the same family for more than ninety-six years. It is one of the longest continually operating newspapers in the Texas Panhandle.

Although Wellington is not "on the beaten path," it continues to sustain its population with an economy now based almost totally on cotton and peanuts. The town is justifiably proud of its museum, the Collingsworth County Museum. The museum and the Collingsworth Art League host a large collection of Sumi ink drawings that are accompanied by interesting descriptions written by the local artist and poet. These alone are worth a stop.

Interesting artifacts housed in the museum include one of the first car tags in the county. It is a homemade leather license plate with aluminum numbers. Another unusual exhibit is a Texas Highway Department vignette, complete with original Highway Department books and tools. Original barbed wire from the line fence of the Rocking Chair Ranch is on display, as well as two items belonging to the famous 1930s bank robbers, Bonnie and Clyde.

The Bonnie and Clyde escapade has been told and retold throughout the years and has made Wellington a place to visit for those interested in these notorious criminals. The Pritchard family was sitting on their porch in 1933 when suddenly a new Ford coupe roared over the hill in front of their house. The car missed a detour at the top of the hill, which was to take them over the Salt Fork of the Red River. Instead, the car followed the unpaved road and plunged into the river.

The Pritchards, some two hundred yards away, rushed to the burning wreckage and doused the flames inside the car with water from the river. The two men in the car began taking from the wreckage what appeared to be guns. The elder Pritchard insisted that the three people be taken into his home where burns suffered by the woman, Bonnie, could be treated. The man offered to drive into Wellington where he could summon a doctor, but the injured trio refused medical attention.

**THE RED RIVER PLUNGE
OF BONNIE AND CLYDE**
ON JUNE 10, 1933, MR. AND MRS. SAM
PRITCHARD AND FAMILY SAW FROM
THEIR HOME ON THE BLUFF (WEST) THE
PLUNGE OF AN AUTO INTO RED RIVER.
RESCUING THE VICTIMS, UNRECOGNIZED
AS BONNIE PARKER AND CLYDE AND
BUCK BARROW, THEY SENT FOR HELP.
UPON THEIR ARRIVAL, THE LOCAL
SHERIFF AND POLICE CHIEF WERE
DISARMED BY BONNIE PARKER. BUCK
BARROW SHOT PRITCHARD'S DAUGHTER
WHILE CRIPPLING THE FAMILY CAR
TO HALT PURSUIT. KIDNAPPING THE
OFFICERS, THE GANGSTERS FLED.
BONNIE AND CLYDE WERE FATED TO
MEET DEATH IN 1934. IN THIS QUIET
REGION, THE ESCAPADE IS NOW LEGEND.
(1975)

The Pritchards soon learned that the three individuals were Bonnie Parker and Clyde and Buck Barrow, fugitives from the law, but it didn't mean much to them. They hadn't heard about this group of desperados who were sweeping Oklahoma, Texas, and Kansas, robbing banks and leaving a heavy trail of blood.

A family member managed to slip away from the house and drive into Wellington for help. He found the sheriff and chief of police and led them back to the farmhouse, where the fugitives "got the drop" on them. The Barrow gang then took the law enforcement officers, bound by their own handcuffs, and sped toward Oklahoma. Shortly after crossing the Oklahoma state line the gang was met by other outlaw friends.

The notorious gang usually killed their victims, but this time they showed mercy and simply stopped the getaway car and tied the officers to a cottonwood tree with barbed wire cut from a fence. The sheriff and chief of police survived the incident and Bonnie and Clyde continued their spree until they were killed in an ambush on a dusty Louisiana road in 1934.

This one accident at the Red River crossing still remains a topic of conversation among old-timers; and it is exciting to visitors when they learn about the Bonnie and Clyde adventure. Tourists traveling on Highway 83 can pass over the bridge, though not the original, and still see the farmhouse where the three took refuge. The county-owned Pioneer Park, near where Bonnie and Clyde crashed, is a popular visitor's site with a playground, two pavilions, and sixteen RV campsites.

The small town of Wellington is certainly off the beaten path, but remains an active and vital part of the eastern Panhandle. The town's activity center is an amazing, bustling community center, complete with six bowling lanes, two basketball/tennis/volleyball courts, a rock-climbing wall, a weight room, racquetball court, two batting cages, an aerobics room, computers with Internet access, and a gymnasium with seating for six hundred people.

The town has a municipal golf course, a Baptist encampment, a swimming pool, lighted baseball fields, a fairground, and an airport. The historic Ritz Theater is currently being restored and will reopen as a movie house and theater for live performances.

This page, left: This aerial view of the Quail area looks like a quilt made with various shades of green. Photo by Kirby Campbell

This page, right The annual Collingsworth County Rodeo brings hopeful contestants and visitors to the county. Photo by Kirby Campbell

Opposite page, top: What could be more typical of the Texas Panhandle than this colorful scene of a windmill and barbed wire at sunset in Collingsworth County. Photo by Norbert Schlegel

Opposite page, left: Irrigation plays an important role in crop production throughout the dry, arid Panhandle. Photo by Kirby Campbell

Opposite page, right: Bull snakes are indigenous to the area and are beneficial because they eat mice, rats, gophers, and small mammals. They are scary looking, but they are not poisonous. Photo by Karen Copeland

Several area ranches host hunters each season, with game hunting becoming a vital part of the county's economy. People come from all over the nation to hunt deer; one of the largest deer ever shot in the state of Texas was shot on a ranch near Wellington. Turkey, quail, and wild hog are also abundant in the county.

More than 2,275 people live and work in Collingsworth County, with Wellington home to most of the population. Other towns in the county include Dodson, Dozier, Samnorwood, and Quail.

Dallam  C O U N T Y

The sister counties of Dallam and Hartley are the heart and soul of XIT country. Dalhart, Texline, Hartley, and Channing comprise a vital, progressive county and one of the most magnificent agricultural production areas in the world. The pioneer spirit that gave birth to these rural towns is alive and well, as evidenced by successful, aggressive businesses covering a diverse spectrum.

The sister counties are located in the northwest corner of the Texas Panhandle and enjoy the unique characteristic of being located at a crossroads with four other states: New Mexico, Colorado, Kansas, and Oklahoma.

Dalhart, the county seat of Dallam County, is home of Texas' first free county library, the first wind erosion station for the United States Department of Agriculture, and the largest free barbecue in the world. The famed barbecue takes place during the world famous XIT Rodeo and Reunion, a celebration of the county's XIT Ranch heritage.

The area is the state's top producer of corn and wheat and the cattle and hog industries are thriving as well. The dairy industry is also growing and quickly becoming another important component of the agricultural economy.

There is much to do in XIT country. The historic LaRita Theater, which was profiled on *CBS Sunday Morning,* offers local community productions as well as touring performances. The XIT Historical Museum chronicles the area's pioneer past and offers changing exhibitions of historic and artistic merit. Nearby Lake Rita Blanca recreational area offers a beautiful retreat for water enthusiasts, bird watchers, and nature lovers alike.

August brings the excitement of the rodeo, tourists, class reunions, barbeque, and money to Dalhart when the XIT Rodeo and Reunion takes place. This annual event is held the first weekend in August and is a three-day festival of nonstop fun and great food. Dalhart is host to the world's largest free barbecue, one of the area's largest street parades, nightly dances, a Professional Rodeo Cowboys Association

The area is the state's top producer of corn and wheat. Photo by Becky Asher

Top: Clowns cavorting during an XIT Rodeo. Photo courtesy of the Dalhart Chamber of Commerce

Bottom: The annual XIT Rodeo and Reunion brings thousands to Dalhart each August. Photo by Johnny Petty courtesy of the Dalhart Chamber of Commerce

Top: The young and the old enjoy making music during the XIT Rodeo. Photo by Kristene Olsen courtesy of the Dalhart Chamber of Commerce

Bottom: The competition is fierce at the annual XIT Rodeo. Photo courtesy of the Dalhart Chamber of Commerce

rodeo, and performances by famed country and western musicians. Grandparents, cowboys, kids, and visitors all enjoy the western flavor of this special weekend.

The XIT Museum offers a taste of the pioneer West through historical and period exhibits, farming and ranching displays, and extensive photographic documentation of bicounty history. The museum partners with local schools and art teachers to offer a visiting artists program. A new and interesting area features wildlife indigenous to the area, some that are rare, and also includes interactive exhibits.

Just down the road north of the Highway 87 underpass is Dalhart's Empty Saddle Monument, in memory of the ranch hands who worked the XIT Ranch. The monument was designed by local artist Bobby Dycke and built in 1940.

The beautiful Rita Blanca National Grasslands encompasses more than seventy-seven thousand acres in Texas, along with almost sixteen thousand adjacent acres in Oklahoma. The protected grasslands attract visitors who hike, bird watch, hunt, ride horses, use off-road vehicles, picnic, or simply enjoy the outdoors.

Nearby Rita Blanca Park was once the northernmost state park in Texas, but is now owned and maintained by the City of Dalhart. It is a prime recreational spot for anyone who enjoys the great outdoors. The park has a 150-acre lake surrounded by 1,668 acres of fun. The lake is an excellent location for birding throughout the year; during the winter months, it is beyond compare.

There is something for everyone in Dalhart, including lovers of the arts. The spectacular La Rita Performing Arts Theater is elegantly restored. Its 1930s period restoration offers community theater productions and other performing arts events. It was originally built and used as a movie theater and still boasts "love seats" for two. Today the lovely old theater hosts live productions throughout the year.

A drive through Dalhart offers a dichotomy, picturing both the old and the new. The stately Dallam County Courthouse stands majestically in the amiable and historic downtown area and is surrounded by a neighborhood of small older homes—some stucco, some clapboard, and an occasional brick veneer. These houses are typical of rural Texas in the 1940s and 1950s and are often banked by tall vibrant hollyhocks and trumpet vines marching brightly along the fence rows, up the telephone poles, and in and out of the lush trees. Lovely old homes and fashionable new designs intermingle in a charming promenade of history. Many homes have been designated as historical landmarks, and beautiful, historic churches abound as well.

Blocks away, the neighborhoods boast worn red brick streets built by the WPA that were new and the pride of the city during the 1940s. The courtly brick streets are wide and often covered with a canopy of trees grown together and touching high overhead. The homes are stately, well kept, and have a certain Southern flair.

A pickup truck seems to be a necessity in Dalhart, whether parked in front of a small clapboard house or a mansion. Dogs, too, are an integral part of the landscape and are often seen riding in the back of a pickup truck or riding "shotgun" with the driver.

The history of Dalhart and the famed XIT Ranch is well known and revered statewide. Although Dalhart was platted in 1901 and briefly called "Twist Junction," its roots are actually much deeper, dating back to 1885 when the XIT Ranch was the largest fenced range in the world. Its three million acres sprawled from the Old Yellow House headquarters, near what is now Lubbock, Texas, northward to the Oklahoma Panhandle in an irregular strip that was roughly thirty miles wide. The XIT covered portions of ten counties, helping perpetuate the false belief that the brand XIT stands for "Ten in Texas." The brand, in fact, was designed as one difficult to alter, therefore discouraging cattle thieves.

XIT history is a triangle of superlatives. The XIT range was the largest in the world under fence. Texas, the biggest state in the Union, used the sale of the ranch

to pay for its red granite capitol, still the largest state capitol on the North American Continent. After more than a century, the Austin structure still houses the Lone Star State's government and, as capitols go, is second in size only to the one in Washington, D.C. In one respect it is even bigger than the United States Capitol because its dome stands seven feet higher.

The XIT was originally created when the Texas Constitutional Convention set aside some three million Panhandle acres to be used for funding a new state capitol. When a

fire destroyed its existing state capitol, Texas made a deal with the Farwell brothers of Chicago whereby they would build a granite Capitol building for Texas in exchange for receipt of the three million acres.

By 1885 the first cattle, long of leg and long of horn, rolled onto the XIT. Thousands of hooves drummed up the trail and the longhorns were pushed onto the Number One Division headquarters at Buffalo Springs, thirty-two miles north of Dalhart. At one time the ranch had more than 150,000 head of cattle. The corrals, foreman's house, and bunkhouse built at the Springs still stand as the oldest structures in Dallam County—a visible tribute to the county's ranching history.

Opposite page, top: *Veterans Memorial Park decorated for the season.* Photo courtesy of the Dalhart Chamber of Commerce

Opposite page, bottom: *Colorful wildflowers blanket the Dallam County prairies.* Photo courtesy of the Dalhart Chamber of Commerce

This page, top: *Veterans Memorial Park in the early summertime.* Photo by Kristene Olsen courtesy of the Dalhart Chamber of Commerce

This page, bottom: *A large arch welcomes visitors to Dalhart.* Photo courtesy of the Dalhart Chamber of Commerce

Deaf Smith

COUNTY

Deaf Smith County is deeply rooted in cattle and agriculture, and its county seat, Hereford, actually derived its name from the Hereford cattle that were brought to this area in 1898. Fed by two underground aquifers, Hereford is well known for its abundant crops of wheat, corn, milo, alfalfa, and cotton.

It is better known, however, as the "Cattle Feeding Capital of the World," with more than three million cattle fed within a fifty-mile radius of Hereford each year. A drive through and around Deaf Smith County offers amazing sights. Hundreds of thousands of cattle are calmly eating and sleeping their way to their final destination on the family dinner table in the county every day, and the "smell of money" is always in the air.

The county's dairy industry is burgeoning and enhances the economy and commerce of the area. It is a natural addition to cattle country. There are twelve producing dairies, with more on the drawing board. The open spaces and arid climate are considered to be ideal for dairy production.

Hereford is located in the western Texas Panhandle at the intersection of U.S. Highway 60, which extends coast to coast, and U.S. Highway 85, which stretches from Canada to Mexico. With an altitude of thirty-eight hundred feet above sea level and a mean temperature of fifty-seven degrees, Hereford has an ideal climate and the wide-open plain is perfect for the raising and feeding of cattle. The excellent transportation system contributes to the diverse economy.

A short drive from Hereford to the east is Palo Duro Canyon State Park; to the north is Lake Meredith; and to the west, the beautiful Rocky Mountains of New Mexico. The metropolitan cities of Amarillo and Lubbock are just a hop, skip, and jump away.

Tourism is alive and well in the town of fourteen hundred. The Deaf Smith County Museum preserves the rich heritage of the community by depicting how pioneers lived, worked, and played. Indian artifacts show evidence of the first

Cattle in Hereford's United Beef Producer Feedlot in 1971. The Hereford steer is in the foreground and Hereford/Angus cross in the background. Photo courtesy of Rebecca Wells

residents of this area. Arrowheads, pottery, and tools from a private collection are part of the museum's display. The museum is housed in a schoolhouse built in 1927.

The museum's outdoor display area is enriched by a completely furnished replica of the first home in the county, a half-dugout. There were no forests to supply lumber or rock for building, so the pioneers "dug in." These dugouts proved to be more than adequate for life on the open prairie. The outdoor area also boasts the county's original metal jail. Although not much larger than an outhouse, the old jail was an imposing structure to outlaws of the time.

The E. B. Black House is a Texas Historical Landmark and is an adjunct to the Deaf Smith County Museum. It was built in 1909 by the E. B. Black family and served as the family's home until 1972, when it was given to the Historical Society. The home is beautifully restored and has lovely, well-cared-for gardens, complete with a gazebo. It is available for tours and provides a nostalgic atmosphere for weddings, receptions, or class reunions.

Left: The E. B. Black House was built in 1909 and is entered in the National Register of Historic Places. It is an adjunct to the Deaf Smith County Museum. Photo courtesy of the Deaf Smith County Museum

Above: Deaf Smith County Museum is a stately red brick building that was originally a Catholic school built in 1927. Photo courtesy of the Deaf Smith County Museum

The Deaf Smith County Library houses more than seventy-nine thousand items that include books, videos, audio books, magazines, and newspapers. It has also become an Internet rest stop for tourists because of its eight free computers with high-speed Internet connections.

Hereford's stately Deaf Smith County Courthouse is notable, not only for its majestic beauty, but because it is the only all-marble courthouse in Texas.

Recreational opportunities abound in this growing community. Hereford's Aquatic Center is one of the finest facilities in West Texas. It is enjoyed year round, with heated water and an inflatable dome cover. Nearby Dameron Park and Veterans Park offer abundant shade and facilities for outdoor fun. The John Pitman Municipal Golf Course is an eighteen-hole course that is a favorite in the Panhandle and host to the Tierra Blanca Golf Classic, which is held the third week each May.

The Spicer Gripp Rodeo Arena is a state-of-the-art facility that was built entirely with private funds. The facility was named for Mr. Gripp, a local roping cowboy who loved the rodeo. The Spicer Gripp Memorial Roping event is held annually, with proceeds donated to the rodeo programs at nearby West Texas A&M University and Texas Tech University. The event is held in August and draws more than two thousand people to the week of activities.

An enterprising dentist once gave Hereford the moniker "the town without a toothache" because of the excessive natural fluoride in the water. People came from all over Texas to have dental work done in "the town without a toothache." An article in *Reader's Digest* about the water and the moniker made Hereford widely known.

The history of the county begins in 1876. It was created from Bexar Territory and was attached to Oldham County for legal and court purposes. Tascosa was the county seat. At this time the only legal protection for the county's citizens was a small ranger force in Amarillo. The ranchers tired of going the long distance to Tascosa to conduct their legal business and, in the summer of 1890, the people of Deaf Smith County signed a petition to become an independent county. The request was granted and the county was organized. The exact center of the county was chosen for the county seat and was named LaPlata.

By 1898 the Pecos and Northern Texas Railway started west from Amarillo to Roswell, New Mexico and came across the southeast corner of Deaf Smith County. The residents of LaPlata understood the importance of the railroad and elected to move the town to the place where Hereford is now. Nine buildings, including the Deaf Smith County Courthouse and the jail, were moved by loading them on wagons and hauling them across the prairie. The town was originally named Blue

---

This page left: Check out the "Sunday-go-to-meeting" clothes at the Deaf Smith County Celebration held on the Courthouse lawn in 1909. Photo courtesy of the Deaf Smith County Museum

This page middle: A lettuce cigarette company called Bravo Smokes was in Hereford in the 1960s. The company failed when the product was deemed inferior to the tobacco cigarette. Photo courtesy of Rebecca Wells

This page right: Registered Herefords were brought to Deaf Smith County in 1898. The town was named Hereford because of this fine herd. Photo courtesy of Rebecca Wells

Opposite page: The wide-open classroom where soft words and calm instructions teach the value of hard work and the value of land. Photo by Mindy Robins

Water, because the Tierra Blanca Creek's deep water was a beautiful dark blue color.

Also in 1898, G. R. Jowell purchased a beautiful herd of Hereford cattle and brought them to Deaf Smith County. Since there was another town named Blue Water, it was decided to change the town's name to Hereford after these new cattle. Over half of the county was a part of the famed XIT Ranch and housed a headquarters where the foreman and cowboys lived.

Deaf Smith County was named for Erastus "Deaf" Smith. Erastus was born in New York but moved with his family to the Territory of Mississippi in 1798. In 1821 he came to Texas and made his home around San Antonio. He spent most of his time in lone ramblings around that part of Texas. Although he was still a young man, he was partially deaf and soon became known as "Deaf" Smith.

At the beginning of Texas' fight for independence, Deaf Smith was one of the first to join the Texas forces. Since he knew the country so well, he was assigned to scouting duty, and in March of 1836 he was made a commander of scouts under General Sam Houston. On the morning of April 21, 1836, Smith was sent by General Houston to destroy Vince's Bridge, which he did; and on the afternoon of the same day he went into battle with such courage that he won praise from the whole army. He was later made a captain in the Texas Rangers, but soon after retired to Richmond, Texas, where he died in 1837. His monument reads: "DEAF SMITH, THE TEXAS SPY, DIED NOVEMBER 30, 1837."

Although Deaf Smith was a famous Texas hero, he never set foot in what is now Deaf Smith County.

This page, left: Ladies working in the Bravo Smoke Factory. Photo courtesy of Rebecca Wells

This page, top: Hereford's unique aquatic park offers something for everyone and as the sign indicates, is very family friendly. Photo by Randall Webb

Opposite page: Night scene of Hereford's Main Street in the early 1960s. Photo courtesy of Rebecca Wells

Donley  COUNTY

Donley County's history has been written by the lives of Indians and explorers, cowmen and plowmen, preachers and teachers, business leaders and laborers. Today this area is the culmination of the dreams of the pioneers who settled here and saw not a formidable wilderness, but rather a land of promise.

The 929 square miles that became Donley County were first only a small part of the Great Plains territory that was roamed by Native Americans for centuries. Unlike the flat "Staked Plains" to the west, this area was, and is, a joy for the eye to behold. The prairie breaks unexpectedly into rugged canyon lands and beautiful tapestries of cliffs and rocks inhabited by a wide variety of flora and fauna. From west to east, Donley County is bisected by the Salt Fork of the Red River; and Texas' own Grand Canyon, the Palo Duro, occupies part of the southwest section of the county.

The Apache were the first people to walk this land. Later, the Kiowa and Comanche claimed the area as part of their homes, and one small group would settle for a time near the banks of the Salt Fork, only steps from where there would one day be a great reservoir.

The area was explored by Spanish expeditions that left only a few scattered relics to mark their presence, and the Republics of Mexico and Texas did little to establish control over this area during their reigns. But America followed a more active path in pursuit of its Manifest Destiny. Captains Randolph B. Marcy and George B. McClellan surveyed the area as part of the U.S. Army's exploration of the Red River, and the government waged the Red River Wars in 1874 and 1875 to subdue the red man. One battle occurred in Donley County in September 1874 when Lieutenant Frank D. Baldwin and a scout were ambushed by Cheyenne on Whitefish Creek in the northeastern section of the county.

Once the natives were confined to reservations, Texas took this part of the Bexar District in 1876 and designated it as Donley County in honor of Stockton P. Donley,

The Donley County Courthouse was built in 1890 and beautifully restored in 2003. The Courthouse is built in the Romanesque Revival style and is asymmetrical, with no two faces being alike. This "Jewel of the Plains" is the oldest functioning courthouse in the Panhandle.
Photo by Norbert Schlegel

a former Texas Supreme Court justice. That same year, Colonel Charles Goodnight drove sixteen hundred head of longhorn cattle into the Palo Duro and brought the beginnings of Anglo settlement to the county. In 1877, he partnered with Irish aristocrat John Adair. Together they established the JA Ranch, which at one point would cover 1,325,000 acres, encompassing most of southwestern Donley County and parts of five other counties.

Later in 1877, a Methodist minister and three companions ventured into Donley County. Like those before them, they found a land rich with wildlife and tall grasses. And like other pioneers, the minister had his own vision of what this land could sustain—a Christian colony where the virtues of temperance and education would reign supreme. The following spring Reverend Lewis H. Carhart secured 343 sections and established a town site at the junction of Carroll Creek and the Salt Fork. He named the settlement Clarendon in honor of his wife, Clara. Soon it was buzzing with settlers from the North and East, most of whom were highly educated and seven of whom were retired Methodist preachers. To promote his colony, Carhart established the *Clarendon News* on June 1, 1878, and gave the Panhandle its first newspaper.

Clarendon was the third Anglo settlement in the Panhandle. Mobeetie and Tascosa were first and second; but, unlike the Wild West lifestyles of its predecessors, Carhart's colony held fast to its founder's ideals. Drinking and gambling were banned, and religion and education were the priorities of the day. So pious was the colony that nearby judges sometimes sentenced lawless cowboys to a short period of time there. Soon the town became known as the place where the saints roosted, and it has been nicknamed "Saints' Roost" ever since.

This page: This white-tailed deer is an example of the many and various kinds of wildlife found throughout the Panhandle. Drivers beware! Photo by Darryl Maddox

Opposite page: The rich prairie grasses and fertile soil were the first siren songs for settlers to the Panhandle. Photo by Darryl Maddox

Also in 1878, an Englishman named Alfred Rowe settled farther down the Salt Fork and established his RO Ranch. Rowe's operation would grow to cover 100,000 acres, and he would later employ many notable cowboys, including the famous African-American, Matthew "Bones" Hooks. Tragically, Rowe's life was cut short in 1912 when, after a trip back to his native country, he was among those who perished in the icy waters of the Atlantic when the *Titanic* sank.

In 1882 Donley County was officially organized, and in 1887, the Fort Worth and Denver Railway made its way through the Panhandle. The route missed Clarendon by six miles, so the town was moved to a new site. "New Clarendon" bore little resemblance to the old town. The railroad brought saloons and other worldly temptations. But, at its heart, Clarendon was still Saints' Roost and it wasn't long before the virtues Carhart had trumpeted would return.

A public school opened in 1888 and Clarendon earned another nickname, "The Athens of the Panhandle," when the territory's first college was opened in 1898 Clarendon College prospered as a Methodist school, became a full senior college, and conferred bachelor's degrees, before politics in the church conference resulted in its reestablishment as a municipal junior college in 1927. Clarendon College moved to its modern campus in 1968. Today it has more than eleven hundred students and serves eight counties with a variety of liberal arts courses and vocational programs.

Throughout its history, many native sons of Donley County have made their mark on the world, including the renowned Western artist Harold Bugbee, whose murals adorn the Panhandle-Plains Historical Museum in Canyon, Super Bowl

record-setter Kenneth King, and United States Representative William "Mac" Thornberry.

Now, more than a century after its settlement, Donley County is easy to get to and offers visitors a variety of attractions. Interstate 40 crosses the county's northern border, and U.S. 287 and State Highway 70 intersect in Clarendon, which is sixty miles southeast of Amarillo. Lake Greenbelt is just six miles north of Clarendon on Highway 70 and has provided fishing, camping, and water sports activities since 1968. Overlooking the lake, the Clarendon Country Club offers an eighteen-hole golf course with an excellent reputation. The native wildlife brings hunters and birdwatchers to the county, and several local guides are available for spotting whitetail deer, mule deer, Rio Grande turkey, quail, duck, geese, dove, coyote, feral hog, pheasant, and aoudad sheep.

The Bar H Dude Ranch brings visitors from as far away as Europe. Three generations of the Hommel family have worked this land northwest of Clarendon, where visitors can sit back and enjoy the scenery or take a horseback ride across the rolling prairie. The Bar H is the perfect place to hold a family reunion or to just get away from it all, and a visit there wouldn't be complete without a delicious mesquite-grilled steak, followed by homemade cobbler.

The Sandell Drive-In Theatre, located in Clarendon on Highway 70 North, is one of the few drive-in theatres still operating in the state. The latest Hollywood hits are shown there every Friday and Saturday nights during the warm seasons.

Clarendon also is proud of the 1890 Donley County Courthouse, which underwent a $4.2-million restoration in 2003. This "Jewel of the Plains" is built in the Romanesque Revival style and is asymmetrical, with no two faces being alike. It is the oldest functioning courthouse in the Panhandle, and visitors are always welcome.

The Saints' Roost Museum is located just off Highway 70 South and exhibits relics of Native Americans and Anglo settlers. The museum is housed in the former Adair Hospital, which was built in 1910 to provide care for the JA cowboys, as well as for the local population.

This page, left: Cornelia Adair, JA Ranch owner, had this hospital built in 1910 to provide medical care for the JA Ranch cowboys. The historic Adair Hospital today houses the Saints' Roost Museum. Photo courtesy of the *Clarendon Enterprise*

This page, middle: The eighteen-hole golf course at the Clarendon Country Club is a popular attraction and provides excellent views overlooking Lake Greenbelt. Photo courtesy of the *Clarendon Enterprise*

This page, right: This massive Longhorn bull whose ancestors roamed the Republic of Texas, proudly symbolizes the unique characteristics of the Texas Panhandle. Photo by Darryl Maddox

Opposite page: Built in 1893, the Church of St. John the Baptist is the oldest Episcopal church in the Panhandle and is among Clarendon's many historic churches. Photo courtesy of the *Clarendon Enterprise*

Clarendon is also home to several state historical sites, including the oldest Episcopal and Catholic churches in the Panhandle and the oldest Methodist congregation. The city also lays claim to the Panhandle's oldest African-American church. The S. W. Lowe House is an example of Clarendon's several historic homes, and other historical markers can be found around the county.

Several annual events bring visitors to the city each year. The Saints' Roost Celebration is held each July to commemorate America's independence and features a ranch rodeo, the Shriners' Barbecue, a turtle race, and a parade. In September the museum hosts the Colonel Charles Goodnight Chuckwagon Cookoff, which features authentic cowboy cooking and pays homage to the local pioneer who created the chuck wagon.

Down the road from Clarendon on US 287, is the community of Hedley where each October locals celebrate the Cotton Festival with class reunions, good food, a parade, and the crowning of the Cotton Queen. In December the community of Howardwick, located north of Greenbelt Lake, gets so serious about holiday lighting that homes there can be seen for miles.

Although Clarendon College, some light manufacturing, Lake Greenbelt, and tourism are contributors, agriculture remains the driving force in the county's economy. Cattle ranching is still predominant, and cotton has long been the king crop. Local farmers also produce an abundance of peanuts and alfalfa, along with grain sorghum and wheat.

With a population of 3,765, Donley County was one of the few rural counties in Texas that actually grew in the last census, and a drive through Clarendon shows several new or recently expanded businesses. With excellent local school systems, a growing college, and several local attractions, Clarendon and Donley County provide ample opportunities for any visitors who want to come stay a day, stay a night, or stay a little longer.

This page: The S. W. Lowe House, built in 1904, is on the National Register of Historic Places and has been maintained in pristine condition by loving patriots of the Panhandle. Photos by Sylvia Lindley Frazer

Opposite page, top: The ranch rodeo is one of the highlights of Clarendon's Saints' Roost celebration each Fourth of July. Also included are turtle races, a barbeque, and parade. Photo courtesy of the *Clarendon Enterprise*

Opposite page, bottom: Beautiful Lake Greenbelt provides visitors with fishing, camping, boating, and other outdoor recreational activities. Photo courtesy of the *Clarendon Enterprise*

Gray COUNTY

Once a part of the Bexar District, Gray County was carved out in 1876 and named for Peter W. Gray, an attorney and politician. The county is located in the central Panhandle and occupies 934 square miles of rolling river breaks and level prairie. The county has immense reservoirs of oil and natural gas as well as soil that supports abundant wheat, corn, grain sorghum, and hay.

Prehistoric Indians roamed the area and were known as Plains Apache. Next were the Apache, who in turn were displaced by the Comanche and Kiowa. These tribes ruled the Panhandle until they were defeated in the Red River War of 1874. These displaced Indians were then moved to Indian Territory in nearby Oklahoma.

Ranchers began coming into the county in 1877. Perry Lefors established a small ranch on Cantonment Creek and other small ranching operations soon followed.

The Francklyn Land and Cattle Company had purchased a large expanse of land that included the western part of Gray County. The company met its demise in 1886 and was reorganized as the White Deer Lands Trust of British Bondholders. This company operated the enormous Diamond F Ranch. A ranching economy with little need for manpower developed in the area and cattle ranchers reigned supreme for the remainder of the nineteenth century.

Gray County was officially organized in 1902 with Lefors as its county seat. The tiny ranching town held on to its county seat status until 1928 when nearby Pampa's oil- induced growth caused it to become the new county seat.

Farmers began coming to the county at the turn of the century and White Deer Lands Company began to sell its prodigious holdings. The land rush to the area of Gray and Carson Counties had begun. The county's population grew with newly arriving farmers settling in the western and northern parts of the county. They planted wheat, corn, and grain sorghums on the newly broken, fertile soil. Farming and ranching dominated the county's economy for a short time; then petroleum discoveries changed everything.

Springtime at the historic Buckler Home in Pampa. C. P. Buckler, manager of the White Deer Land Company, built the house in 1915. Photo by Loralee Cooley

Oil and gas exploration began in the early 1920s and a major discovery well was found just five miles south of Pampa. Other wells were drilled, leading to more developments in the county. The mid-1920s brought increasing amounts of oil out of the county's three oil fields. Production escalated and by 1929, the county had become a major player in oil production. A by-product of the oil economy was a large petro-chemical industry that produced carbon black and other synthetic materials.

Pampa, the primary beneficiary of the oil boom, emerged as the center of the growing industry. The county seat and largest town in the county, Pampa is located in the northwestern part of the county, sixty miles east of Amarillo. The town was named Pampa because of its resemblance to the pampas of Argentina.

An early settler, Timothy Dwight Hobart, envisioned the area as a wheat belt and, with the help of two associates, attracted many prospective settlers to Pampa. The new town soon thrived and became a small agricultural and railroad shipping point, populated largely by homesteaders and cowboys. The discovery of oil in 1926 caused a population explosion in Pampa and its future was assured in 1927 when Cabot Carbon Company of Boston established the first of several carbon black plants nearby.

World War II brought about the Pampa Army Air Field and filled the town with servicemen and their families. The war and its aftermath spurred more industrial growth. The Columbian Carbon and Coltexo Companies and the Celanese Corporation of America built plants in the vicinity, as did the Skelly, Phillips, Shell, and Kerr-McGee oil firms. The population increased more than 100 percent from 1941 to 1960. The Chamber

Top: One of the area's many oil derricks lights up the night sky in Gray County. Photo by Norbert Schlegel

Bottom: A new day is born as a blazing Panhandle sunrise illuminates an exploratory oil rig. Photo by Daryl Maddox

of Commerce and local Economic Development Board advertised Pampa as the "Friendly City at the Top O' Texas, Where Wheat Grows and Oil Flows."

Pampa offers tourists a variety of ways to look into its history and enjoy the community. The White Deer Land Museum contains that company's records and documents in addition to pioneer artifacts. This museum boasts one of the Southwest's largest individual arrowhead and primitive tool collections.

Hobart Street Park, named for early settler Timothy Dwight Hobart, provides free campsites and hookups and is a popular place for families to gather.

Military enthusiasts flock to the Freedom Museum USA. This unusual and interesting museum features military memorabilia including a Bell UH-1F Huey Helicopter and an M110A2 Howitzer.

Another unusual Pampa museum is the Woody Guthrie Museum. Guthrie, a dustbowl balladeer, lived in Pampa for a short time and later wrote many memorable songs, including the well-known *This Land Is Your Land*. Woody was an influential and prolific American folk musician, noted for his identification with the common man, the poor, and downtrodden. He was a lifelong socialist and trade unionist and contributed a regular column, "Woody Sez," to *The Daily Worker* and *People's World* newspapers. Guthrie, describing himself, said "I am nothing more nor less than a photographer without a camera." The museum features Guthrie memorabilia and is a work in progress.

Nearby Lefors is twelve miles southeast of Pampa in central Gray County. The town was named for Perry Lefors, who became the first town constable. Despite

Dust Bowl of 1936. The Panhandle was devastated by drought, wind erosion, and great dust storms. The Dust Bowl caused great ecological and economic disaster.
Photo courtesy of
Norbert Schlegel

its small size and the lack of a railroad, the town managed for a time to remain the county seat. Three oil pools were discovered in the vicinity during the 1920s and Lefors profited from the boom.

Another neighboring town, McLean, was first established as a cattle loading pen site on the Rock Island Railroad in 1900. Alfred Rowe, an English rancher, donated the rangeland site. Rowe later died on the *Titanic* in 1912.

McLean began to grow when Congress commissioned Highway 66 in 1926. Route 66 was born and the spirit of the hardy pioneers lived on. For the people traveling the road in search of a better life, the Texas Panhandle brought many hardships, as well as kinship with the locals who helped them along the way.

The pre-66 road was dirt, very crooked, and had square turns as it followed section lines and crossed and recrossed the Rock Island Railroad many times across the Panhandle. The road was there first, and when the railroad was built in 1910 to 1911, the grades required many crossings of the old road. As the road was improved, eventually Old 66 was built, and most crossings were eliminated.

Travelers on Old 66 in the early 1930s probably averaged sixty miles per day, if they didn't break down or get stuck in the thick Panhandle mud. Many locals made extra spending money by assisting travelers out of muddy roads with teams of horses.

Everyone carried the essential watering can. If the kids didn't need it, the car would. Gas stations were not modern and seemed hard to find. Oklahoma-based Phillips Petroleum Company built its first Texas service station in McLean in 1927. The motel or tourist court hadn't been invented and hotels were rare and expensive. Many people camped just where night caught them.

There are 178 miles of the Old 66 road across the Panhandle. It is a trip back through time to travel the road, remembering those who have gone before, many times in broken-down cars and trucks, always hoping for an easier life somewhere down the road. Tourists feel the warm Panhandle winds and observe the immenseness of an area that to some was "as vast as the ocean."

It's springtime in the Panhandle. Early blooming lilacs surround the First Presbyterian Church of Pampa. Photo by Loralee Cooley

World War II brought the McLean Enemy Alien Internment Camp to McLean and German prisoners of war taken in the North African Campaign began arriving in early 1943. The camp eventually housed more than three thousand prisoners.

McLean, like its Gray County neighbors, boomed with the discovery of oil. However, through the years, agriculture has remained its most stable source of income.

The revival of Route 66 brought on renovations of several vintage Route 66 sites and new business in McLean surged. McLean became the permanent home of the Texas Old Route 66 Association, which established the first Route 66 Museum on the "Mother Road," with its offices in the new museum complex.

Visitors are intrigued by the restored Phillips 66 Service Station, the old Avalon Movie Theater, and the unique downtown district. The McClean/Alanreed Area Museum features local history of the McClean POW Camp, and depicts the impact the POW Camp had on the town. The actual campsite is just north of town and is complete with a Texas Historical Marker.

The Devil's Rope Museum is a fascinating trip through the area's past and is the largest historical barbed wire museum in the world. Local lore has it that Indians called barbed wire "devil's rope," thus the name of the museum. The museum is all about the history of barbed wire, its artifacts, the significance of the invention, and its impact on the development of the Old West. Vignettes depict entanglement wire used in warfare, a monument dedicated to barbed wire, the history of cattle brands, an exhaustive early tool collection, and information about Texas Route 66. Another interesting exhibit features actual Burma-Shave signs that were used along the highways during the mid-1900s.

A complete deviation from barbed wire is a vintage paper doll exhibit that delights the hearts of girls from six to eighty-six. Handmade quilts are also on display.

There is much to do in Gray County. It is diverse and offers something of interest for everyone.

A large collection of windmill heads make an interesting display on the Chapman Ranch just outside of McLean. These heads are not just for show. Workers use parts to fix or replace other heads as needed.
Photo by Dick Frazer

Top left: Barn owls have a white, heart-shaped face with large dark eyes. They are great rodent hunters and are found throughout the Panhandle. Photo by Sydna Stout

Top right: Yellow wild flower. Photo by Daryl Maddox

Middle: Beautiful pond on the Chapman Ranch. Photo by Karen Chapman

Bottom left: Pasture scene at sunset. The barbed wire and cedar post is near the Devil's Rope Museum in McLean, which features a large collection of barbed wire. Photo by Norbert Schlegel

Bottom right: Acres and acres of colorful wildflowers bloom on the George and Karen Chapman Ranch in Gray County. Photo by Sylvia Frazer

Hall  COUNTY

Hall County is located in the southeastern Panhandle, east of the High Plains and about 90 miles southeast of Amarillo. The county is 885 square miles of rolling plains and broken terrain, crossed by the Prairie Dog Town Fork of the Red River, the Little Red River, and many smaller tributaries.

Apachean people lived and worked in the Panhandle-Plains area in prehistoric times. In more recent times, the modern Apache were pushed from the region around 1700 by the Comanche, who were the undisputed rulers of the Panhandle-Plains, including Hall County. The Red River War of 1873–74 ended in defeat of the Comanche by United States soldiers. The Indians were subsequently removed to Indian Territory in 1875–76.

The Texas legislature divided lands formerly designated to Bexar and Young Counties and formed Hall County in 1876. The Indians were quickly replaced by buffalo hunters as they moved across the Plains between 1877 and 1882. In just five short years, the buffalo in Hall County were annihilated.

Cattlemen followed the buffalo hunters, and a number of major ranching operations moved into the area. In 1876 Charles Goodnight and John Adair established the huge JA Ranch, which, though headquartered in Armstrong County, spilled over into several surrounding counties, including Hall. By 1890 seventy-nine ranches and farms had been established in the county and the population had increased to 703. The large ranches were eventually divided and sold to land-hungry pioneers for individual family farms.

In most Panhandle counties the railroad played a major role in the development of the area; Hall County was no exception. Construction of the railroad and organization of the new county made Hall County attractive for settlers. By 1910 there were more than one thousand farms and ranches in the county and the local economy had been transformed. The number of people living in Hall County almost quintupled between 1900 and 1910, growing to more than eight thousand.

Parts of many movies are shot in the Panhandle because of sunrises and sagebrush just like this.
Photo by Norbert Schlegel

The agriculturally based economy continued to flourish until the Great Depression of the 1930s. The census recorded almost 17,000 people living in Hall County in 1930. The Depression hit the Hall County farmers in a hard way, with the county losing more than a third of its farms in the ten-year period between 1930 and 1940. The county's population dropped to 12,117 by 1940, as dust-blown farm families left the land and moved elsewhere.

Today Hall County is again humming, but with a soft, slow buzz. Memphis remains the county seat, with Turkey, Estelline, and Lakeview adding to the core of the county's population.

Two major attractions bring tourists to Memphis. The Presbyterian Building has been designated a Texas Historic Landmark and is available for private tours. The massively beautiful old church was built to last forever in 1911, from brick fired in the Memphis kiln. It features neoclassical revival detailing in the use of arched windows and a domed roof. Seventy-three beautiful European stained glass windows, both plain and portrait, cover every window. Interior furnishings include a large pipe organ, originally powered by water pressure and later electrified. All of the interior wood surfaces, including the organ, are solid oak. A child-sized church was built in the basement in the late 1920s and provided a special place for children to worship. The beautifully constructed Presbyterian Building is a "must-see" when in Hall County.

Another tourist "must" is the Land Company. This interesting company builds primitive furniture, which is then hand-painted by a local artisan. The company occupies more than a city block in Memphis' downtown area. People come to Memphis from all over the nation to visit and order from the Land Company. A uniquely lovely restaurant is open for lunch with the master builder and painter often acting as chef.

The Hall County Heritage Hall Museum stands proudly on Main Street, one of more than ten miles of red brick streets in the beautiful, historic town. The Memphis

From left to right:

The former Presbyterian Church in Memphis has been designated a Texas Historic Landmark and is available for private tours. The massively beautiful old church, designed after St. Peter's Cathedral in Rome, was built in 1911. Photo by Mary Lenderman

The majestic pipe organ in the church is made of solid oak and was originally powered by water pressure. Photo by Mary Lenderman

The former Presbyterian Church has seventy-three beautiful European stained-glass windows, both plain and portrait. Photo by Mary Lenderman

The church was built from brick fired in the Memphis kiln and features neoclassical revival detailing in the use of arched windows and a domed roof. Photo by Mary Lenderman

The Hall County Courthouse sits proudly in downtown Memphis. The style is Texas Renaissance. Photo by Mary Lenderman

The Hall County Heritage Hall Museum is easy to find on a corner on Main Street in Memphis. Photo by Mary Lenderman

The Depression hit farmers in a hard way. Hall County lost more than a third of its farms between 1930 and 1940. Farmers Lona Lee and Samuel L. Lindley are seen here circa 1936–1940. Photo courtesy of Sylvia Lindley Frazer

Bob Wills Reunion, honoring the King of Swing, is held annually the last Saturday in August in Turkey, Texas. Photo courtesy of the *Valley Tribune* and Vince and Laura Taylor

City Park is complete with a creative playground, walking track, camper and RV hookup, and the oldest amphitheater in the state.

The annual Hall County Reunion is held the third Saturday in September and kicks off with a cowboy breakfast. The day includes a parade, a poker run, a barbecue and, finally, dancing on the Square.

Another major tourist attraction in Hall County is Turkey, the home of the King of Swing, Bob Wills. The Bob Wills Museum is a fascinating attraction to music lovers everywhere. The museum honors the musician, who was reared on a farm just north of the town. Memorabilia of the Texas Playboys and of Wills' career and its influence on American music is displayed. The famous musician is also recognized with a monument at the west end of Main Street.

The Bob Wills Reunion is held annually the last Saturday in August. Each year thousands of music lovers and aficionados of Western Swing throng into the rustic little town of five hundred hardy souls. Although the town's population is small, crowds range from ten to fifteen thousand during the festival.

The historic Hotel Turkey was built in 1927 and has remained in continuous operation. It is listed with the state and national historic registries. Today the hotel is a bed-and-breakfast establishment. Its fifteen rooms retain their original 1927 decor.

Turkey is located in the southwest corner of Hall County, just below the edge of the Llano Estacado. It lies one hundred miles southeast of Amarillo and one hundred miles northeast of Lubbock. The little settlement was originally called Turkey Roost because of the many turkey roosts along Turkey Creek, but the name was shortened when the Post Office was established in 1893. In the early days, wild turkey roosted in the cottonwoods. Coyote, large lobo wolves, black bear, and even panthers roamed the shinnery (dense growth of small trees) in large numbers. The settlers began moving into the county in 1890 and subsequently drove the big game away from this part of the country.

Hansford
COUNTY

The great buffalo hunt, which depleted the huge herds of the western United States, began in the early 1870s. Kansas and Colorado were the first to lose their herds of the magnificent shaggy beasts to hunters; Texas became the next hunting ground.

The buffalo slaughter in Texas began in 1876 and was completed in just three short years. One of the most successful hunters was an Englishman named James H. Cator. It is estimated that Cator himself shot sixteen thousand buffaloes during the years of slaughter. The Cator camp was later moved to Paladura (Palo Duro) Creek in today's Hansford County in 1873. Adobe Walls was used by hunters as a supply point while they searched the top of Texas for fresh hides.

Brothers James and Bob Cator made their lifelong home along the Paladura Creek in Hansford County. They built a pole building from native cottonwood and called it the Zulu Stockade. The Zulu name came from a British war that was being fought in Africa at the time. In 1880 the Zulu Stockade became the first post office and was a trading post on the Dodge City to Tascosa trail. Also among the famous buffalo hunters was Billy Dixon, who favored a prized, rare white buffalo hide. Dixon is also touted as the hero of the Battle at Adobe Walls.

As the buffalo disappeared from the landscape, Hansford County began to take shape, its rolling prairies extending for miles and miles in every direction. Growth continued as farmers moved into the county. Rugged pioneers plowed the land and planted grain by hand. A man could file for ownership of four sections of land as long as he lived on one of the sections and continued to improve all four. He was charged sixteen dollars a section as a down payment and one dollar an acre, with the balance to be paid over a forty-year period at 3 percent interest.

The influence of the railroad was apparent in Hansford County, as in many Panhandle counties in the early 1900s. Spearman was platted in 1917 and named for Thomas E. Spearman, vice president of the Santa Fe Railway. It was then designated as the Hansford County seat.

"Windmillers," history buffs, and schoolchildren travel to Spearman to be amazed by this unusual collection. Photo by Rick Vanderpool

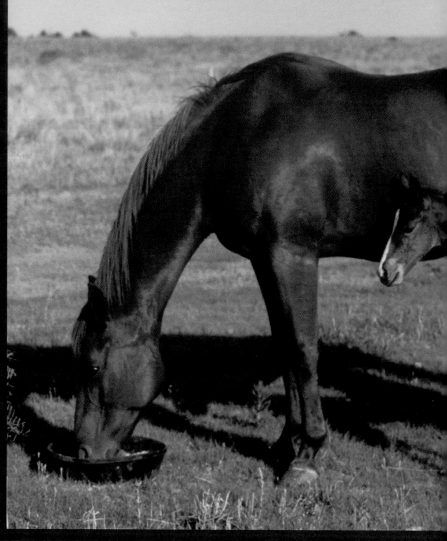

Photo captions and credits, bottom row from left:
Cattle do well in the mild Hansford County winters. As a result, feedlots thrive in the area. Photo by Ann P. Wells

Back roads in the Panhandle, framed by the big sky and miles of power lines Photo courtesy of the Amarillo Chamber of Commerce

This red, white, and blue windmill proudly sports the colors of both the American and the Texas flags. Photo by Rick Vanderpool

Hansford County occupies nine hundred square miles, has a population of more than five thousand, and includes Gruver, Morse, and the county seat, Spearman. Spearman is a vibrant, growing, "micropolitan" town best known as the "city of windmills." The city displays more than fifty windmills of all sizes, shapes, and colors. The J. B. Buchanan Windmill Park, located in the downtown area, was established in 1999 by a group of "windmillers" and community volunteers who worked hard to make it possible.

The Windmill Park is an outdoor museum of sorts, sporting only windmills of functional design. Some are wooden wheels, while others have folding wooden wheels, and some are unusual steel mills. Most were working windmills, lifting water from underneath the earth to provide water for a homesteader's crop or a rancher's livestock. "Windmillers," history buffs, schoolchildren on field trips, folks who have never owned a windmill, and folks who have never even seen a windmill travel to Spearman to see this unusual collection.

Another amazing collection in Hansford County can be found at the Texas Alligator Ranch, located in Spearman, just blocks from downtown. These living descendants of the dinosaurs can be viewed "up close and personal" on a short walking tour through the ranch.

Lake Palo Duro, ten miles north of Spearman, offers area residents and visitors excellent opportunities for recreation on and off the water. The 60,900-acre lake has a shoreline of more than forty-eight miles and an average depth of forty-six feet. Boating and camping are enjoyed for a minimal fee and RV sites with hookups are available. Fishing and birding are also popular at this beautiful, well-maintained lake. The lake is a wintering site for the American bald eagle and other rare bird species.

The famous Adobe Walls Battle site is located thirty miles south of Spearman and Indian artifacts continue to be found in and around Hansford County. There were two battles at Adobe Walls, the first in November 1864 with Kit Carson in attendance; but it was the second battle that contained the "stuff of legends."

Left: The J. B. Buchanan Windmill Park located in the downtown area was established in 1999 by a group of "windmillers" and volunteers who worked hard to make it possible. Photo by Randall Webb

Middle: Spearman is a vibrant, growing, "micropolitan" town best known as the "city of windmills." The city displays more than fifty windmills of all sizes, shapes, and colors. Photo by Randall Webb

Right: The Windmill Park sports only functional windmills. Most have worked hard lifting water from underneath the earth to provide water for a homesteader's crop or a rancher's livestock. Photo by Randall Webb

Spearman's Alligator Ranch is an unusual sight, just blocks from downtown. These living descendants of the dinosaurs can be viewed "up close and personal" while touring the ranch.
Photo by Randall Webb

Buffalo hunters had moved south and west after the decimation of the buffalo herd in Kansas. In 1874 two stores were set up to rekindle the town of Adobe Walls and for shopkeepers to make a few dollars off the hunters. By late June there had been talk of Indian problems and a few hunters had been killed. Some twenty-eight persons were present at Adobe Walls, including twenty-year-old Bat Masterson and Billy Dixon.

Early in the morning on June 27, the pole holding up the sod roof of the saloon broke with a loud crack. People from the town woke early and began to repair the damage, so they were up when, at dawn, a combined force of Kiowa, Comanche, and Cheyenne warriors swept across the plains, intent on killing everyone at Adobe Walls. Comanche Chief Quanah Parker, son of a captured white woman, Cynthia Ann Parker, led the raid of an estimated seven hundred mighty warriors.

The initial attack lasted all day with the Indians at one point close enough to pound on the doors and windows of the buildings with their rifle butts. The fight was in such close quarters the hunters' long-range rifles were useless. After the initial attack was repulsed, the hunters were able to keep the Indians at bay with their Sharps rifles. Fifteen warriors were killed so close to the buildings that their bodies could not be retrieved by their fellow warriors.

The second day a scouting party of the remaining warriors rode out on a bluff nearly a mile away to look over the situation. Billy Dixon, a crack shot, took aim and cleanly dropped a warrior from his horse. This apparently so discouraged the Indians that they gave up the fight and fled.

The history of Hansford County is interesting and the rugged beauty of the area is a delight for both the naked eye and the shutterbug.

Hartley COUNTY

One cannot talk about Hartley County without also talking about Dallam County and the famed XIT Ranch. Hartley and Dallam are more than sister counties; their histories are so entwined that they can be called "kissing cousins."

Located in the northwestern part of the Panhandle and bordered on the north by Dallam County, Hartley County consists of 1,488 square miles of flat to rolling grasslands. The topography is distinguished by jagged, dry arroyos and the Punta de Agua and Rita Blanca Creeks, which come together in Hartley County and drain into the Canadian River in adjoining Oldham County. The county's elevation reaches up to 4,200 feet above sea level.

The frontier reached Hartley County in the 1870s. The region was a very small part of the vast, empty High Plains, which extended from Texas to Canada. An Apachean culture inhabited the area from prehistoric days, but they were driven out of the area by the Comanche who ruled the territory until 1873–74, when they were finally defeated in the Red River War. They were then moved out of the county to Indian reservations in Oklahoma.

In 1876 The Texas legislature gave land formerly designated to Bexar and Young Counties to Hartley County. The new county began to develop in the early 1800s as the county changed from raw frontier into the kingdom of the rancher. A huge ranching industry was developing in Northwest Texas and after the Civil War many ranches were established in Hartley County. The famous XIT Ranch was formed along the western border of the Panhandle in 1882 and occupied a large part of Hartley County. The XIT Ranch was once the largest fenced range in the world. Its three million acres sprawled from the Old Yellow House headquarters, near what is now Lubbock, Texas, northward to the Oklahoma Panhandle in an irregular strip that was roughly thirty miles wide.

Channing, the county seat of Hartley County, is located on the Fort Worth and Denver City Railway in the southeastern part of the county. Many towns in

Sunflowers are one of the newer cash crops of the Panhandle. Photo by Roy Lane

the Panhandle claim association with the vast XIT Ranch, but only Channing can truthfully say that it developed directly from the XIT. In 1891 the general headquarters of the XIT was situated in Channing. The ranch's general manager built the first house in the town. It was called, Boyce's "Poor Farm" and was located at the Rita Blanca Division headquarters, less than two miles south of town. The original XIT headquarters remains in Channing and is a popular visitor site.

The small community of Hartley bears the name of the county. Situated fourteen miles southeast of Dalhart, Hartley began as a tent village in 1888. The town was elected as the county seat, but soon lost that designation to Channing.

When the town of Tascosa was abandoned, several of its businesses moved to Channing. Two elections were required for Channing to replace

---

This page, top: Day is done on beautiful Lake Rita Blanca. Photo by Randall Webb

This page, right: A cowboy's spurs were necessities in the early West. Photo courtesy of the Panhandle Plains Historical Museum

Opposite page, top: Thousands of geese enjoy some R&R at Lake Rita Blanca. Photo by P. J. Pronger courtesy of the Dalhart Chamber of Commerce

Opposite page, middle: The original XIT headquarters remain in Channing and are a popular visitor site. Photo courtesy of the Dalhart Chamber of Commerce

Opposite page, bottom: A Hartley County windmill is framed by the windy sunset. A storm is brewing in the late spring. Photo by Norbert Schlegel

Hartley as the county seat. Channing eventually won out and the original frame Hartley County Courthouse was moved from Hartley to Channing on wheels by XIT cowboys. The frame structure became a hotel when the brick Courthouse was built in 1906. Just two years later, the local women's club established one of the earliest public libraries in the Panhandle in the old frame Courthouse.

The XIT Ranch continued to conduct most of its business from Channing until liquidation of the ranch in 1911. The land was sold off to create smaller ranches and farms, causing a real estate boom. Ranching and farming remains the base of Hartley County's economy today.

Again, to talk about Hartley County is to talk about Dallam County and the XIT Ranch.

Hemphill COUNTY

Hemphill County is one of the most beautiful counties in the Texas Panhandle. It is rife with trees and verdant vegetation. Red Deer Creek and Lake Marvin add water to the mix and the result is splendid!

Canadian, the only town in the county, is its county seat. Its population is slightly more than twenty-five hundred, but the ambiance of the community makes it seem much bigger, more metropolitan. The downtown area is alive and bustling with renovations and the sounds of progress. This lovely old community retains its historical charm, while enterprising citizens renew, rework, and renovate its old buildings.

A leisurely drive through Canadian is a pleasant, sensory experience. The colors, the smells, and the sights are almost too much to take in on a first drive through the area. This river city is awash with opportunity for family fun and a chance to revel in what one writer called being "a million miles from Monday." Taking a walk to enjoy the historic, nostalgic downtown district or a drive to view the mesas of the Canadian River Breaks ranch country and observe the flora and fauna of its pristine, short grass prairie make for an unforgettable experience.

The High Plains loop of the Great Texas Wildlife Trails provides passage to sixty-eight regional wildlife-viewing sites, twelve of which are in the Canadian area. Birding and wildlife enthusiasts prospecting for a look at fauna such as bobwhite quail, burrowing owl, prairie dog, and the lesser prairie chicken can take advantage of the year-round viewing opportunities.

Located in the lush Canadian River Valley, Canadian has a long tradition of sheltering visitors weary from the trail. Visitors today join the ranks of Native Americans, soldiers, cowboys, gold miners, and pioneers who made their winter camps in the valley, enjoyed this oasis of water and shade in the summer months, and, finally, railroad, highway, and air travelers who have found the small town a modern "oasis" away from the demands of urban workday life. Many of those

Reflections of Lake Marvin. This beautiful sixty-three-acre lake in Hemphill County is truly nature's showcase. Photo by Betty Pugh

travelers decided that this Panhandle valley was the place to make a home and a history. They had arrived at their destination and built warm homes where families are cherished, history is valued, and small town living is at its best.

Travelers to Canadian find much to do and see, and an afternoon drive through town will simply not do. Although the environs are eye-candy for the soul, a more active look is often desired. There is great energy in Canadian. Main Street has been transformed with the restoration of once vacant buildings into thriving establishments. New businesses have opened and existing ones are expanding and upgrading.

While downtown, visitors may enjoy a delicious Texas-style meal at the beautifully restored Moody Hotel's Cattle Exchange Restaurant and then walk a few blocks on brick streets and step into yesteryear at the charmingly restored Palace Theater whose interior whispers of the grandeur of America's Art Deco period. Once a home for vaudeville, the Palace now shows the latest blockbuster hits. After the movie, an ice cream cone at the recently renovated City Drug is in order. The drugstore itself is a history lesson and has been restored in exacting detail to mimic the original apothecary.

Before leaving downtown, the River Valley Pioneer Museum is a "must-see." The Museum opened in 1986 to preserve the rich heritage of Hemphill County pioneers and its turn-of-the-century beginnings. The museum houses many artifacts on permanent display and hosts traveling exhibits in the Gallery Room.

Canadian was recently awarded a federal grant in excess of one million dollars as a part of the state's Main Street project and the funds are being used to build a handsome visitors center.

Entering Canadian from the south on Highway 60, children are delighted to see Aud, the concrete dinosaur who sits atop a mesa on south Highway 60/83. Aud stands guard at the entrance to the Canadian River.

Continuing north out of town, the Canadian River Wagon Bridge is often a visitor's next stop. The bridge, eligible for the National Historic Register, was completed in 1916 and was the largest steel structure west of the Mississippi at that time. It is important because of its service as a local and regional transportation route, as well as being a major engineering accomplishment. The bridge's 1923 trusses are the latest examples of pin-connected metal truss spans in the state. The Canadian River Historic Wagon Bridge not only spans a splendid Texas prairie river, it spans time, transporting the traveler to an earlier era and inviting a slower pace.

A five-year restoration project was completed in 2000 and the Canadian River Wagon Bridge was reopened and is now a part of a scenic hiking and biking trail through the Canadian River Valley and wetlands habitat. The bridge is not only great for walking, biking and jogging, but a fine place for bird watching and wildlife viewing as well.

A short distance northeast of Canadian sits magnificent Lake Marvin, with 575 acres of grassland and riparian areas surrounding a sixty-three acre lake. The twelve-mile drive down a tree-lined road to nature's showcase at Lake Marvin is stunning. Recreational opportunities for fishing, picnicking, overnight camping, hiking, and wildlife viewing abound. The Lake Marvin area is unique in that it offers a common ground for both eastern and western plant species, due to its location between the Canadian and Washita River Valleys in the eastern Texas Panhandle and western Oklahoma.

The wildlife at the lake is as diverse as the plant species. Game species include bobwhite quail, turkey, white-tailed deer, raccoon, opossum, striped skunk, beaver,

From left to right:

Aud, the huge metal dinosaur, has delighted children for years. He is located on a mesa south of Canadian. Photo by Gayle Haygood

The historic Moody Building in Canadian was built in 1910 as the Moody Hotel. Today, the restored building houses the Cattle Exchange Restaurant and the Abraham Investment Company. Photo by Gayle Haygood

The beautifully restored Palace Theater sits prominently on Canadian's Main Street. The street will soon be restored to look like the original brick street. Photo by Gayle Haygood

The Canadian River Bridge. Photo by Norbert Schlegel

Romancing the Texas Panhandle

muskrat, bobcat, and coyote. Waterfowl stop at Lake Marvin during migration and use it as a wintering area as well. Mallard, wood duck, teal, and goose represent some of the waterfowl. There is also a diverse group of shorebirds, passerine and accipitrine, that lives in the area or passes through at times throughout the year. Bald eagle, least tern, and trumpeter swan are a few of the uncommon species seen at Lake Marvin.

The Gene Howe Wildlife Management Area, just a few miles from Canadian, is two-thirds sandsage/midgrass rangeland and one-third cottonwood/tall grass rangeland. It is used for nature research and also available for public enjoyment. Public hunting is one of the primary uses of the Gene Howe area. Public hunts are held for dove, quail, deer, and feral hog in the fall and for wild turkey and feral hog in the spring. The area is also utilized by students, teachers, researchers, and wildlife enthusiasts for instructional and educational purposes.

A primitive camping area is equipped with fire pits and restroom facilities. The Beaver Lodge Hiking Trail is a popular interpretive hiking trail located in the West Bull Pasture on the Gene Howe Wildlife Management Area.

Several bed-and-breakfast establishments dot the county. The Arrington Ranch House and Lodge was a movie location for *Cast Away,* starring Tom Hanks, and serves as a lovely respite for travelers. This working cattle ranch offers not only incredible natural beauty, but also the opportunity to lend a hand with the spring or fall cattle work.

The county hosts several events and activities, the most well-known being the annual Fall Foliage Festival. Mid-October each year finds thousands of nature

Opposite page: This old and mighty cottonwood tree stands on the Shannon Ranch close to Lake Marvin in Hemphill County. Photo by Gayle Haygood

This page: Four horsemen out for a ride are Lee, Glen, and Hollis George and Henry Young. Photo probably taken by Johnny Young (note fifth horse with empty saddle) in 1918 on the Ed George Ranch in southeast Hemphill County on the Gageby Creek. Photo courtesy of Gayle Haygood, daughter of Lee George

and wildlife lovers taking the breathtaking drive through Hemphill, Roberts, and Lipscomb Counties. Bus tours, wagon rides, an arts and crafts fair, a 10k and 5k runs, a brisket dinner, a motorcycle poker run, a ranch rodeo, and a dance are part of the weekend's activities.

Hemphill County is located in the southwest quadrant of the Anadarko Basin, one of the deepest basins in the continental United States, with in excess of forty

thousand feet of sediments. Oil and gas leases were acquired in Hemphill County as early as the 1920s; several wells were drilled and later plugged. Technology had not yet developed sufficiently to explore the depth of the Anadarko Basin production.

By the late 1950s, oil wells were again drilled and producing. Oil and gas exploration and development has contributed to the economy and progress of Hemphill County. Oil-related companies are listed among the major employers in the area. But more than just dollars, the search for oil and gas has enriched the county's history. The real romance began long before a drill bit hit the ground. It was the dreamers and speculators who risked life, limb, and bank account to find this elusive cache that molded the county's tradition of thinking big.

Today, whether your taste runs to first-class restaurants or homey cafes, fine art or hoedown, history or the latest in business technology, nature and wildlife viewing, or unique and interesting shopping, you'll find it all in Canadian.

Opposite page, left: The annual Fall Foliage Festival brings thousands of nature and wildlife lovers to Hemphill County each year. Photo by Darryl Maddox

Opposite page, right: The Canadian River is the largest tributary of the Arkansas River. It rises in the Sangre de Cristo Mountains near Raton and flows south, separating the Llano Estacado from the High Plains. This view was taken from the bridge in Canadian, Texas. Photo by Gayle Haygood

Opposite page, bottom: Aerial view of Canadian shows a colossal landmark in all its glory. Photo by Zane McGee

This page, top left: This handsome private residence is called "The Citadel" and was originally the First Baptist Church of Canadian. Photo by Gayle Haygood

This page, top right: The Women's Christian Temperance Union building in Canadian was built in 1914. Today, the building houses the Hemphill County Library. Photo by Gayle Haygood

This page, middle: Branding the old-fashioned way at the Anderson Ranch in Hemphill County. Photo by Gayle Haygood

This page, bottom: Canadian's traditional Fourth of July Parade is a part of the annual three-day Rodeo Celebration. Canadian has the oldest rodeo in Texas. Photo by Gayle Haygood

Hutchinson  COUNTY

To talk about Hutchinson County is to talk about Indians, artifacts, water, and, of course, oil. As the popular theme song of *The Beverly Hillbillies* television show said, "Black Gold . . . Texas Tea." Hutchinson County and specifically Borger, the "Boom Town," was, and is all about oil.

The county's 871 square miles of broken terrain are situated in the north central section of the Panhandle. Borger is the most populated town, Stinnett is the county seat, and Fritch is a recreation Mecca for the entire Panhandle.

The Antelope Creek Indians lived here in the prehistoric times and artifacts of this culture are plentiful along the Canadian River Valley in Hutchinson County. Apache and warlike Comanche, Kiowa, and Southern Cheyenne also camped in this area. Spanish explorers, Coronado and Onate, rode through in the mid-1500s and early 1600s.

In 1836 a trading post was opened at Bent's Creek, now in eastern Hutchinson County. The post, known as Fort Adobe, operated until about 1842 when trouble with the Indians led to its abandonment. Its ruins later became the site called Adobe Walls. During the 1800s French traders, cibalero and Anlgo buffalo hunters, and *comancheros* traded and hunted in the vicinity.

Cattlemen were the first white settlers in the county and, for the next forty years, ranching dominated the county's economy. In 1890 the county had fifty-eight people living on nine ranches. Hutchinson County's boundaries were established and the county was attached first to Bexar County and then to Roberts County. In 1901 Hutchinson County was officially organized and Plemons was designated as the county seat. Billy Dixon, the Adobe Walls hero, was the county's first sheriff.

Hutchinson County remained sparsely populated until an immense Panhandle oilfield was discovered in 1924. Dozens of oil camps sprang up almost overnight as oil-related industries moved in, and many independent oilmen became instant millionaires. Borger, named for its founder, A. P. (Ace) Borger, was the largest and roughest of these boom towns.

This spring conveys the tranquility enjoyed at Three Falls Cove, a country inn located just north of Lake Meredith National Recreation Area at Sanford, Texas. Photo by John Ward

Railroads responded to the oil boom, coming to the county in 1924. Stinnett became the county seat in 1926 and the population of the county grew from 721 in 1920 to more than 14,000 in 1930 as a result of the big oil bonanza.

The Great Depression, along with the Dust Bowl, ended the boom, but the oil business kept people working. Petroleum prices dropped and by 1930 unemployment in the county began to take its toll. However, Hutchinson County also experienced some prosperity as many migrant workers found jobs in the oilfield, causing the population to reach almost 20,000 by 1940.

The rubber carbon black industry came alive during World War II and Buena Vista, just west of Borger, became the new home of synthetic rubber carbon black plants. In 1943 more than 360,000 pounds of carbon black were produced. The county's population continued to grow and tourism and recreation were encouraged in the 1960s with the building of the Sanford Dam on the Canadian River, which created Lake Meredith.

The sixties, seventies, and eighties showed some decline in petroleum-related industries, which hurt the county's economy. Population continued to decrease until 2005 when energy prices soared and activity in the oilfields cranked up once again. A stable community, centered on oil and gas production and distribution, grew out of the boom-era chaos. Today Hutchinson County is a major American petroleum supplier and an important part of the nation's oil industry.

Borger remains the largest town in the county with a 2006 population of more than thirteen thousand. It is still widely known as "Boom Town" and the Hutchinson County Museum revisits those booming days. The museum depicts life in Hutchinson County from the days of Coronado's expedition in the 1500s through 1969, when Borger was selected as an All American City by *Look* magazine. Perhaps its best-known and most frequently visited exhibits are the scale models of the buildings at Adobe Walls which help reveal the story of the battle that precipitated the Red River War.

Both natives and visitors appreciate the opportunity to get "up close and personal" with an authentic, ninety-five foot cable tool drilling rig. Borger's Derrick

Left: Texas Rangers and inmates. Legendary Texas Ranger Frank Hamer had the policy of "one riot, one Ranger"; however, when he arrived in Borger in 1927, he immediately called for backup. The jail was too small, so prisoners were chained to logs outside. Photo courtesy of the Hutchinson County Museum

Right: Borger's second birthday celebration included this parade on March 8, 1928. "Boogertown" was populated by entrepreneurs—some honest and some not; prostitutes; gangsters; and others all eager to make their fortunes in the new oilfields. Photo courtesy of the Hutchinson County Museum

Downtown Project has changed the skyline of the city and generated excitement throughout the area. It is the most complete rig of its type in Texas and work continues toward making the rig operational. It is located across the street from the Hutchinson County Museum; rig tours are available by appointment.

The Borger Pump Jack Project is a work in progress and will serve to enhance and honor the petroleum heritage of the area. The venue is billed as the "largest collection of pump jacks in Texas." The pump jack represents Boom Town Borger and is a colorful, artistic way to demonstrate how the city has emerged. Converting the old pump jacks of the area to works of art is the heart of this project.

Top: Full-scale drilling rig on display across the street from the Hutchinson County Heritage Museum in Borger. Photo by Darryl Maddox

Bottom: Pump Jacks are a common sight in Hutchinson County. Borger is still widely known as "Boom Town." Photo by Darryl Maddox

Other attractions, unrelated to the oil industry, include an interesting outdoor bird sanctuary hosting thirty to forty different species and the Veteran's Memorial in Huber Park. The downtown movie theater, The Morley, boasts the largest indoor screen in the Panhandle and is the only theater with a balcony. It has been beautifully restored and shows recently released movies on three screens. Two beautiful golf courses, a tournament-sized horseshoe area, an airport with runways long enough for jet landings, and a community college complete with a rodeo program and an activity center with Olympic-sized pool are other areas of local interest.

The county seat, Stinnett, sits proudly in the central part of the county. Its ornate Hutchinson County Courthouse is the largest old courthouse in the Panhandle and is reflective of the riches of the oil boom in the county. It was built in 1928, has sculpted pediments both inside and out, marble hallways, and three complete courtrooms that are still in use.

This small town was not the boom town of neighboring Borger, but greatly benefited from the oil fields surrounding it. Many profiteers looking for "black gold" lived in boxcar shanties and canvas tents, giving early Stinnett its share of lawlessness and violence. During the Prohibition Era many establishments in town

illegally sold whiskey and beer in their back rooms and *rowdy* was a commonly used word for the locals.

Stinnett's interesting museum on the Courthouse Square is the restored 1899 box-and-strip cottage of the area's first settler, Isaac McCormick. This pioneer home was centrally located; the first county meetings and elections were held there; the county was organized there in 1901.

Fritch sits prominently ensconced in two counties, Hutchinson and Carson. It is the home of Lake Meredith, probably the most heavily visited recreation area in the entire Panhandle of Texas. Fritch is the tourist capital of Hutchinson County, featuring numerous things to see and do.

You won't be the first person to discover Fritch; however, people have been there for more than ten thousand years. Fritch was the first great international manufacturing center of North America. The flint from nearby Alibates Quarry has been found in archeological digs from Mexico to Minnesota. Not far from Fritch is a marker that commemorates the great Fort Smith Santa Fe Trail, which passed through the area. The swales from the wagon tracks are still faintly visible from the roadside.

Lake Meredith National Recreation area is a vast forty-five-thousand-acre playground. Recreational opportunities abound, including fishing, hunting, boating, sailing, birding, hiking, biking, swimming, and camping. It is on the northern edge of the Llano Estacado and is perhaps the finest prairie park in the Great Plains, covering canyon lands and grasslands. It is designated as a National Recreation Area rather than as a National Park, and that difference in definition allows consumptive activities, such as hunting, in the area. This recreational lake and the surrounding area are used by as many as one and a half million visitors annually when lake levels are high.

Opposite page: The stocked, spring-fed pond at Three Falls Cove is a surrounded by towering cottonwoods. Photo by John Ward

This page: A beautiful, still summer evening at Three Falls Cove. Photo by John Ward

The lake is the number one walleye lake in Texas and also serves as a source for walleye stocked in other Texas lakes. Hunting occurs year-round, subject to state hunting laws and federal restrictions. Primary game includes whitetail and mule deer, turkey, dove, quail, goose, and duck.

The marina provides a launching ramp and many boaters and sailors keep their boats moored year-round at the marina. Below the dam is the Spring Canyon swimming area and a tract of wetlands that provides opportunities for birders.

The Lake Meredith Aquatic and Wildlife Museum in Fritch provides a look at the local plant and animal life and contains large aquariums that display fish from Lake Meredith.

It's a short drive from Fritch to the Alibates Flint Quarry National Historic Landmark. One could think that the Alibates quarries might be named for an obscure Greek God; however, they were actually named for Allie Bates, a cowboy and local character who used to work along the river.

The quarries produce Alibates flint, an agatized dolomite outcropping of the Permian Age, on both the north and south sides of the Canadian River valley. The flint was used for chipped stone tools from more than ten thousand years ago until the 1800s. The working of Alibates flint could be characterized as one of the earliest and longest-lived industries in early America.

The Alibates Flint Quarries National Monument was created in 1965 to preserve the flint quarries. It consists of 1,079 acres, with hundreds of the quarries and several

Top: The marina at Lake Meredith is the home to all kinds of sailboats and motor craft. Photo by Mariwyn Webb

Middle: Lake Meredith is one of the most visited recreation areas in the entire Panhandle of Texas. Photo by Randall Webb

Bottom: Lake Meredith offers fishing, camping, hiking, water skiing, jet skiing, sailing, and just "chilling out" watching the sunset. Photo courtesy of the Hutchinson County Museum

Above: Alibates flint with quartz crystals. Colors are due to impurities in the rock, red from iron and black from manganese. Photo by Darryl Maddox

*Heavily weathered
Alibates flint
found in the
Alibates National
Flint Quarry in
Hutchinson County.*
Photo by Darryl
Maddox

village sites. Guided tours are presented on a reservation basis by park rangers. A
new Visitor Contact Station has recently been built.

Another point of historical interest is nearby Adobe Walls. This is the site of
two of the most famous battles in the struggle for land between the Southern Plains
Indians and Anglos. Two major battles occurred at Adobe Walls. In 1864 during
the Civil War, the first battle, led by legendary Kit Carson, ended in retreat when
Carson came upon an overwhelming force of more than three thousand Indians. The
second battle occurred in 1874, when a buffalo hunters' trading post was attacked
by a party of seven hundred Plains Indians, under the leadership of Quanah Parker.
The twenty-nine defenders repelled the initial charge with a loss of only three men.
The five-day siege continued as hunters in the vicinity were notified of the attack
on Adobe Walls. By the fifth day there were more than one hundred men at Adobe
Walls. The Indians subsequently gave up the fight and retreated. The battle led to the
Red River War of 1874–75, which resulted in the final relocation of Southern Plains
Indians to reservations in what is now Oklahoma. Monuments were erected in 1924,
1936, and 1941 on the site of Adobe Walls to commemorate the battles.

Hutchinson County has a rich and unique heritage and may be one of the
undiscovered secrets of the Southwest. It is located on the High Plains amid
abundant native cacti, wildflowers, cattle, windmills, and oil wells. Most days
begin with vibrant sunrises and end with brilliant sunsets. The average 326 days
of sunshine each year is envied by many.

Lipscomb COUNTY

"The Panhandle of Texas with its broad, sweeping, fertile prairies, its numerous streams and springs of pure running water, magnificent groves of ash, elm, and cottonwood, is now opened for the settler and the farmer. Already the cabins of the squatters along the creek bank half hidden among the trees and the sod houses of the settlers loom up as castles upon the broad limitless prairie. But they stand lonely and are but the forerunners of the farm houses, the villages, and the cities that will soon ornament every slope and crown every hill. Millions of acres are yet awaiting the homing of the home seeker. Millions of acres of rich alluvial soil that needs but to be turned to the sunlight, and the seeds dropped upon it, to return a bountiful harvest of golden grain," wrote J. M. McDonald when describing Lipscomb County. This poetry of the Panhandle appeared in the *Panhandle Nester,* a newspaper published by McDonald. This enthusiasm and vision for the future of the county was probably shared by all the prairie settlers.

In the heart of the eastern Panhandle sits a quietly serene and breathtakingly beautiful piece of rural Texas. Lipscomb County has five picturesque towns: Lipscomb, Booker, Darrouzett, Higgins, and Follett. The county's population is around three thousand. Lipscomb, the county seat, has a human population of only fifty permanent residents, but is proud of the two hundred turkeys that strut around the Lipscomb County Courthouse and call Lipscomb home.

Lipscomb sits prominently in the center of the county on State Highway 305. In the late 1800s Lipscomb's location in Wolf Creek Valley was thought to be a Valhalla for cattlemen. In 1886, anticipating the arrival of the Panhandle and Santa Fe Railway, Mr. J. W. Arthur opened a combination store and post office at the site. The town was named Lipscomb in honor of a pioneer judge named Abner Smith Lipscomb. The most prominent county developer, Frank Biggers, organized the town company, selling land for three dollars and acre. A heated contest to determine the site for the county seat soon ensued between Lipscomb and the rival town sites of

---

Lipscomb, the county seat, has a human population of only fifty permanent residents, but is also proud of the two hundred turkeys that strut around the Lipscomb County Courthouse and call Lipscomb home. Photo by Karen Chapman

Timms City and Dominion. An election was held the next year and Lipscomb was chosen as the county seat.

Germans from Russia were among the town's early settlers. The town began to thrive and a school district was established. The Alamo Saloon was a popular watering hole until 1908 when the county voted to go "dry."

The "best laid plans oft go astray" and did so in Lipscomb County when the railroad put down its tracks just south of the town. Many attempts to get a railroad to Lipscomb were unsuccessful, leaving the town site "high and dry." A five-inch vein of coal was discovered in the area about this time and local businessmen were also unsuccessful in their attempts to develop a coal mine. The community's position as the county seat, along with several real estate ventures, helped the town to survive, but growth was halted.

Lipscomb's economy has remained stable because of farming, ranching, and oil and gas explorations in the vicinity. Although Lipscomb is the smallest town in the county and is off the main highway with no rail access, it remains the county seat.

Summertime brings tourists and art and music lovers to Lipscomb. The Naturally Yours Gallery and Dance Platform in downtown Lipscomb is the place to be for summertime fun. Families gather for an evening of music under the stars in the town of Lipscomb, where the turkeys outnumber the residents. Music resonates on summer evenings when time-honored fiddler music, mesquite smoke from cook fires, and laughter fill the air.

Art, too, is an important part of the Naturally Yours complex. Every month the gallery features the work of talented artisans, including oil painters, furniture makers, potters, photographers, watercolorists, authors, wood carvers, and songwriters. Locals will remind visitors to remember their lawn chairs, their bug spray, and their good humor!

The Wolf Creek Museum is another popular visitor's site in the fascinating little town of Lipscomb. The museum provides a place of history where young and old alike may visit and learn about their heritage.

Lipscomb's northwest neighboring community of Booker was originally a part of Oklahoma. In 1909 the town was located seven miles to the northwest in La Kemp, Oklahoma. It was moved in pieces and parts from Oklahoma to Texas in 1919 when the railroad

Top: Lipscomb County Courthouse was built in 1916 and stands as a promontory in Lipscomb today. The style is Classical Revival. Photo by Gayle Haygood

Bottom: The Wolf Creek Museum is a popular visitors site in the quaint little town of Lipscomb. Photo by Gayle Haygood

Top: The Naturally Yours Dance Platform and Gallery in downtown Lipscomb is the place to be for summertime fun. Photo courtesy of Naturally Yours Gallery and Dance Platform

Bottom: Summertime brings tourists and art and music lovers to Lipscomb. Photo courtesy of Naturally Yours Gallery and Dance Platform

was extended from Shattuck, Oklahoma, to Spearman, Texas. The new town site was platted and given the name Booker. By 1920 the town was flourishing with a population of more than 600. It boasted of cattle-shipping pens, a school, a bank, grain elevators, and three churches. The Great Depression and Dust Bowl took their toll on Booker, causing the population to decline to 386 in 1940. By 1949 recovery had occurred due to agricultural innovations, new farming techniques, and oil exploration and the population climbed to more than 1,500. After 1956 the town greatly benefited from local oil and gas production. Today Booker is the largest town in Lipscomb County and is again experiencing a boom in the energy sector.

Each spring brings fiesta time to Booker. This fiesta celebrates the Mexican lifestyle and features live entertainment in an all-day celebration.

Darrouzett was settled in 1917 in the northern part of Lipscomb County. It began as a station on the Panhandle and Santa Fe Railway and was platted at the junction of Kiowa and Plummer Creeks. The original town name was Lourwood, named after the first child born there. The rail line was completed in 1920 and the town was renamed in honor of Texas legislator John Louis Darrouzett, who served as an attorney for the Santa Fe Railway. Businesses and settlers moved to Darrouzett from the Sunset community in Oklahoma to be near the railroad, and the town was soon incorporated. During the 1940s and 1950s Darouzett became "the best paved town per capita of the Panhandle," at a cost of $80,000. The population has remained stable.

An annual cultural event in Darrouzett, Deutsches Fest, brings visitors to have some fun and to enjoy the pastoral ambiance of the town. This German (not Dutch) festival is held annually on the first Saturday in July. It is a celebration of the town's German heritage and includes a melodrama, parade, baby contest, mustache

contest, and noon meal of German sausage and accoutrements. Another Darrouzett celebration is the annual Buzzard Bash, held to celebrate the migration of buzzards in the spring. It features breakfast, a chili cook-off, an egg hunt, and the crowning of the Buzzard Queen and King.

Just two miles south of the Oklahoma border sits Higgins, Texas. It is located on U.S. Highway 60 in the southeastern part of Lipscomb County, in the heart of the North Texas grasslands of the early cattle ranges. The area has been associated with a Franciscan monk named Juan de Padilla, who came to the area with Francisco Vazaquez de Coronado. Padilla later returned to work among the Indians and was martyred in 1544. The actual site of Padilla's missionary work remains unknown.

Settlement of the rural site began in 1886 when the railroad made inquiries into the area regarding extension of its branch line. The town was named Higgins after G. H. Higgins of Massachusetts, a wealthy stockholder of the Santa Fe Railway. By 1888 area ranchers had made the town a major shipping point. In 1898 nineteen-year-old Will Rogers came to Higgins and worked for a while on the Little Robe Ranch. The burgeoning town was incorporated in 1908 and won a considerable reputation as a

Left: Bear grass, often called Yucca, blooming against the backdrop of the vibrant Lipscomb sky. Photo by Norbert Schlegel

Above: Hundreds of trees in a rare frosted state. Photo by Zane McGee

Opposite page, middle: Bobcats still roam the region. They look like the lynx, but are smaller with a more heavily spotted coat. They are bold stalkers of small game. Photo by Sydna Stout

Opposite page, bottom: Cottontail rabbits are found not only in the outlying pastures but also in towns, and are favorites of children. Photo by Roy Lane

progressive community. The citizens are a resilient lot and have weathered depressions, dust storms, and cyclones. The drought in 1885 and 1886 was so devastating that an early settler wrote on a board nailed across the door of his cabin: "250 miles to the nearest post office. 100 miles to wood. 20 miles to water. 6 inches to hell. God bless our home. Gone to live with the wife's folks." The town's worst disaster occurred in 1947 when a tornado claimed forty-five lives and devastated the business district and several homes.

Today Higgins is a grain and livestock marketing center and is also the beneficiary of oil drilling in the immediate area. In 1962 the town began an annual observance of Will Rogers Day, in honor of the cowboy philosopher.

Last, but not least, of the five Lipscomb County towns is Follett. It is located on State Highway 15 in northeastern Lipscomb County and was established in 1917 by a Santa Fe Railway official. It was named for Horace Follett, a Santa Fe engineer. The town became an overnight success when the citizens of Ivanhoe, Oklahoma, moved their businesses and homes across the state line to be near the new railroad. The population grew to 550 and Follett was incorporated in 1920. The Farmers Grain Co-op soon made the new town a wheat and grain sorghum storage and distribution center and helped it gain its nickname, "Gateway to the Golden Spread." Like the other towns in Lipscomb County, Follett flourished because of grain, cattle, oil, and gas.

Lipscomb County is a true gem in the eastern Texas Panhandle.

Moore
COUNTY

Moore County is aptly named because it truly is "more county." The area is vast
and the industry diverse, resulting in Moore County's steady growth. Dumas, Sunray,
and Cactus are the communities within its nine hundred square miles.

A drive into Dumas on Highway 287 gives a visual picture of rural America. The
land is flat, the cactus and wildflowers abound in vivid hues. The cows are grazing,
the pump jacks are pumping, and the sun is shining through the mist of circular
irrigation stations. Depending on the day, you may see a lone cowboy riding the
range checking his fences. Another day a cowboy may be on a four-wheeler rounding
up his cattle. You can be sure that both cowboys are wearing a Stetson hat and have a
cell phone attached to their belts.

You can almost hear the steady hum of progress as you enter Dumas from the
south. You'll see progress as you pass the new Wal-Mart Superstore on your right.
A quick look to the left and you'll see the Window on the Plains Museum and Art
Center. A leisurely drive through town gives you a true sense, not only of America,
but of rural Texas.

Dumas has the traditional stately courthouse you'll see in many Texas county
seats. It is built of brown brick and invites tourists to use their cameras. The town is
spotted with thriving businesses, banks, car washes, and fast-food eateries. Charming
antique stores line Main Street. Tourists look for and find the "Texas Stop Sign," The
Dairy Queen, for a hamburger and a Dilly Bar. Here one can see the character lines
on the faces of men, young and old, as they lean on the backs of their pickup trucks
and talk over the day. These guys are affectionately called "Ding Dong Daddies" and
are a part of the legend and lore of the town of Dumas.

The "Ding Dong Daddy" moniker has a long history, beginning in the late 1800s
when Louis Dumas brought his family to settle on the raw prairie in the upper
northern part of the Panhandle. Dumas and other hardy settlers were drawn to the
Panhandle because of its wide-open spaces, cheap land, and the opportunity to make
something out of nothing. Louis Dumas and a partner, J. Turner Wilson, bought two

Wildflowers light up the pasture on the Brent Ranch in Moore County. Photo by Sylvia L. Frazer

sections of land from the Houston and Texas Railway for slightly more than $3,500 and formed the Panhandle Townsite Company.

Thirty-two eligible voters banded together in 1892 and approved bonds for the Moore County Courthouse, and the organization of Moore County began. The town fathers were visionary in their thinking and platted much wider streets than most other small towns so that Dumas escaped traffic problems as growth occurred. Louis Dumas busily promoted the new town while running a farming and ranching operation. He became one of the county's first commissioners and later a justice of the peace.

Heavy snows and fierce winds blew into Moore County in the winter of 1894–95, killing thousands of cattle. A few years earlier, a drift fence had been built to keep the cattle from wandering. This same drift fence caused their demise as they headed south away from the icy winds, were trapped by the fence, and froze to death. "The cattle huddled to keep warm but every head froze where it stood. One could walk on dead cattle for miles," remembered Mrs. Walton, daughter of Louis Dumas.

The Window on the Plains Museum is a stellar attraction in the county with numerous displays centered on ranching, farming, wildlife, Plains Indians, and vignettes depicting the early settlers' life in the county. Photo by Randall Webb

The deadly winter had ravaged Louis Dumas' farm and ranch operation and in the spring the family returned to East Texas. Louis Dumas, visionary and developer, had created a town and put his personal stamp on the land. The town was ultimately named after him and he became its first "Ding Dong Daddy."

Dumas, the town, struggled on, growing slowly with farming and ranching as its economic base. Then in the early 1940s the discovery of oil and gas gave the area a much-needed shot in the economic arm.

Dumas' population was nearing six hundred in the late 1920s when Phil Baxter came upon the little town. He made a stake, stayed a while and then moved on to become a band leader. The people of Dumas had made a lasting impression on Mr. Baxter and less than a year later, he wrote a song he titled "I'm a Ding Dong Daddy from Dumas."

Phil Baxter later became Jack Benny's band leader and his little ditty about the "Ding Dong Daddy from Dumas" gained some national recognition. The Benny Goodman Trio, the Louis "Satchmo" Armstrong Band, and Arthur Godfrey all recorded Baxter's song about Dumas.

Dumas residents soon organized and began operating a radio station and the song became its signature song. They named the station KDDD; the three "Ds" came from the title of "I'm a Ding Dong Daddy." A logo was created; lapel pins were fashioned and have been handed out to thousands of visitors over the years. The "Ding Dong Dollies" were added in later years.

A heavy snow like this one and fierce winds blew into Moore County in the winter of 1894–95, killing thousands of cattle. Photo by Daryl Maddox

Today Dumas is a bustling, growing town of more than twenty-one thousand. For some, the bright lights and big city beckon. Others soon grow weary of the glitz and glamour of metropolitan life. For those individuals, Moore County offers the perfect alternative. It is nestled in the heart of the Texas Panhandle and offers a unique meld of attractive location, competitive wage structure, a highly skilled work force, low cost of living, and an unparalleled quality of life. You'll find hardworking people in Moore County. Their work ethic is strong, as is their sense of family and tradition, their faith is steadfast and they welcome with open arms their new neighbors, who soon become old friends.

With agribusiness at the core, the area has a strong, sound, diversified economy. The county's hub, Dumas, is joined by the smaller communities of Sunray and Cactus. The air is clean and there's no such thing as a traffic jam.

Photo captions and credits clockwise, from bottom left:
Moore County farm southwest of Dumas. Photo by Kathy Dickman

Treasure Island Water Park in Sunray boasts a seventy-five-hundred-square-foot pool, two twenty-foot-tall water slides, palm trees, a pirate ship, a whale slide, water volleyball, and more. Photo by Kathy Dickman

American Legion Post 224 Memorial proudly flies American flags to honor war veterans. Bricks with names of people who have lost their lives in U.S. wars lead up to the memorial. Photo by Kathy Dickman

The traditional stately Moore County Courthouse. Photo by Randall Webb

This dandelion parachute is just about to take off and seed the pastures. Photo by Darryl Maddox

The Disaster Memorial in front of the Moore County Courthouse is dedicated to those who gave their lives in the Diamond Shamrock-McKee Refinery explosion in 1956. Photo by Randall Webb

The lone hawk perches atop the windmill, getting a bird's-eye view of the county. Photo by Norbert Schlegel

RAY BILES
LEWIS A. BROXSON
O. W. SHINE CLEVELAND
GILFORD CORSE
BILLY JOE DUNN
CLAUDE L. EMMETT
ALVIN W. FREEMAN
SAM A. GIBSON
DURWOOD C. LILLEY
CHARLES W. LUMMUS
OLIVER MILLIGAN
PASCHEL POOL
JAMES L. RIVERS
M. WAYNE SLAGLE
WAYNE THOMAS
DONALD W. THOMPSON
GAYLE D. WEIR
RUEBERT S. COTTON WEIR
JOE W. WEST

BUT WHETHER ON THE PLAINS SO HIGH
OR IN THE BATTLE'S VAN,
THE FITTEST PLACE WHERE MAN CAN DIE
IS WHERE HE DIES FOR MAN.

DEDICATED TO THOSE WHO GAVE THEIR LIVES
IN THE MOORE COUNTY DISASTER ON

Moore County has much to offer its visitors. The region offers a wealth of outdoor activities, such as boating, skiing, and fishing at nearby Lake Meredith and hunting all over the county. The Cactus Playa Lake just northeast of Dumas is a treasure trove for bird watchers and nature lovers.

The beautiful Window on the Plains Museum is a stellar attraction of the county. It opened in 1976 as Moore County Historical Museum and was housed in the ballroom of an old hotel. Philanthropists, history lovers, and volunteers worked hard to create a permanent home for the collections and in 2001 the project was completed and the name changed to Window on the Plains Museum. There are numerous displays centered on ranching, farming, wildlife, and Plains Indians, and vignettes depicting the daily life of the early settlers in the county.

Adjacent to the museum is the Art Center that was built as a neighbor and companion to the Museum. The Art Center features exhibits that change monthly of area artists' works and houses workshops to help from beginners to the most accomplished artists hone their skills. An extensive permanent collection of oils, watercolors, acrylics, sculpture, and other media by Texas Panhandle artists is on display. The Museum and Art Center are located on ten acres at the southwest corner of Dumas on Highway 87-287.

Summer brings tourists and class reunions to Dumas for the annual Dogie Days celebration. The four-day festivities include a parade, carnival, midway, barbecue dinner, and prize drawings. You can take a romantic horse-drawn carriage ride or enjoy a wagon hay ride for up to twenty people.

Nearby Cactus, Texas, holds an annual Diez y Seis Celebration each September fifteenth through the seventeenth recognizing Spanish Independence Day and featuring a parade, carnival, crafts, and live music. Cactus is home to Swift and Company Beef and Cactus Feeders.

Sunray, Texas, another integral part of Moore County, is home to the incredible Treasure Island Water Park. This public water park boasts a seventy-five-hundred-square-feet pool, two twenty-foot-tall water slides, palm trees, a pirate ship, a whale slide, water volleyball, and soft play animals for the enjoyment of county residents and tourists alike.

Moore County, Texas—nine hundred square miles of clean air, big sky, and starry nights.

See ya there!

This page: Campers at Lake Meredith enjoy a beautiful Moore County sunrise. Photo by Kathy Dickman

Opposite page: The Cactus Playa Lake just northeast of Dumas is a treasure trove for bird watchers and nature lovers. Bald eagles can be spotted throughout the area. Photo by Karen Copeland

Ochiltree COUNTY

Ochiltree sounds like the name of an indigenous tree known only in the Texas Panhandle. Or it could be a nocturnal animal that sleeps in the tops of mesquite trees. However, those things it is not. Ochiltree is a county in the northernmost part of Texas, seven miles south of the Oklahoma state line. Its unusual name came from a Republic of Texas judge named William Beck Ochiltree. Judge Ochiltree was also Confederate secretary of the treasury and an officer in the army of the Confederacy.

The county was created thirty years after Texas was admitted to the Union, but it would take another thirteen years for it to be officially organized. Perryton is the county seat and is today a bustling, growing city of more than nine thousand. Its history and that of Ochiltree County are among the most interesting histories of the Wild West.

In 1919 the Santa Fe Railway was building a rail line from Shattuck, Oklahoma, westward and the residents of Ochiltree began making extensive efforts to have the railroad run through their town. However, there were problems with this plan. If the railroad built the line within five miles of a county seat, it was required to run part of the route through the town. The costs of building the track through the banks of Wolf Creek proved to be prohibitive, and, for these reasons, the railroad chose not to run tracks through the town.

The savvy business leaders of the town knew the importance of being close to the railroad and decided that if the railroad would not come to them, they would go to it. The towns of Ochiltree, Texas, and Gray, Oklahoma, decided to merge and move their homes, businesses, churches, and other buildings to the present site of Perryton. This was a huge task in 1919 and garnered national attention. Buildings, some with families inside, were literally picked up off their foundations and moved across the prairie to the new county seat of Perryton on specially constructed wagons pulled by pairs of dapple-grays and a steam engine. At times, some of the two hundred homes were chained together and moved as one to increase the efficiency of

Beautiful Lake Fryer offers a plethora of water sports, while the land lover can choose from a wide selection of hiking trails. Photo by Gayle Haygood

the relocation. The entire move took only a few weeks to complete. Today the only thing that remains of the old town of Ochiltree is one schoolhouse and a historical marker. The town was renamed Perryton in honor of George M. Perry, a pioneering citizen who served as county clerk for many years.

There is much more to the history of the region than the moving of towns for the railroad. One of the most spectacular finds in archeology, and one of its best-kept secrets, exists just outside of Perryton. Known as the "Buried City," this Indian ruins area is rich in clues to the lives of the earlier inhabitants of this area.

In 1907 a professor at the Canadian Academy took one of his classes to investigate the area. They discovered a two-mile stretch of Indian ruins running along the Wolf Creek Valley. Discoveries have continued for nearly a century. The findings puzzled early archeologists. They knew the site was not a Plains Pueblo site from the New Mexico Indian cultures, yet neither was it a typical Plains Village site. Today scientists still agree that it was neither, and that is what makes the site so unique. Work to understand the site and to uncover more answers continues today on what is now the private ranch of the Courson family.

The rich history of Ochiltree County is available to anyone with an interest in history. A walk through the Museum of the Plains provides insight into the past. It is a journey through thousands of years of life on what is commonly called "The Great American Desert." The area, rich in history, is also called "No-Man's Land" and "The High Plains. Well-done exhibits portray the Dutcher Ranch mammoth as well as the centuries-old Buried City at Wolf Creek. More than ten thousand artifacts chronicle the history of civilization up to the current age.

Ochiltree County is the hub of recreation and tourist attractions in the area. Wolf Creek Park and Lake Fryer are located off Highway 83 near Perryton and offer a variety of activities for the entire family. You may camp in the same places as the early frontiersmen and enjoy the

Top: A walk through the Museum of the Plains in Perryton provides insight into the past. It is a journey through thousands of years of life on what is commonly called "The Great American Desert." Photo courtesy of the Perryton Chamber of Commerce

Bottom: Beautiful Lake Fryer and Wolf Creek Park are located off Highway 83 near Perryton and offer a variety of family activities. Photo by Gayle Haygood

Area beauties pose in a wheat field in the mid-1940s. All are hoping to be chosen as "Wheatheart of the Nation." Photo courtesy of Sydna Stout

quiet beauty of nature just as they did. The lake also offers water sports, while the land lover can choose from a wide selection of hiking trails. Wolf Creek Park is a favorite camping spot, with ninety-four RV hookups providing full electricity and water. Picnic tables and barbecue grills also dot the shaded campground. For the more primitive camper there are several wilderness areas scattered around the lake, inviting the camper to pitch a tent. Both the north and south shores have bathhouses with hot showers and restrooms.

Fishing in the well-stocked lake is a popular area activity. A variety of fish are stocked annually. Boating, swimming, wind surfing, and skiing can also be enjoyed. The park's interesting trails are full of flora and fauna, including deer, antelope, turkey, and many other species of native wildlife. The Lobo Trading Post provides camping needs, permits, memorabilia, and a good dining experience. The Fourth of July is celebrated each year with a spectacular fireworks display. Wolf Creek Park and Lake Fryer are two of the finest recreational areas in the entire Texas Panhandle.

Each August the Wheatheart of the Nation Celebration takes place in Perryton. The event celebrates the founding of the city and marks the day the first train steamed through Ochiltree County in 1919. Festivities begin with a breakfast followed by a parade commemorating the founding of the city. The Museum of the Plains offers free admission to the museum during this celebration and patrons can browse through booths set up by local artisans.

The Perryton Municipal Golf Course is home to the annual Oil Patch Golf Tournament which draws players from all over the region. The eighteen-hole course, lighted tennis courts, municipal swimming pool, and other recreational activities are all available to guests of the city.

Area motorcycle enthusiasts look forward to the annual Texas Vietnam Veterans Memorial Highway Motorcycle Run. The four-day event honors the men and women who served their country in Southeast Asia. Riders travel Highway 83 from Perryton to the Veterans International Bridge in Brownsville, Texas.

Perryton celebrates the traditional Mexican holiday of Cinco de Mayo. The May 5 festival commemorates the region's strong Mexican heritage with food and fun, including a dance.

Perryton is the gateway to Texas for travel and business. Located just minutes from Oklahoma and less than an hour from Kansas, the city enjoys year-round visitors from many states.

Perryton has natural beauty with wide-open spaces and clean, clear air. Vast wheat farms have earned the county its well-deserved title as "Wheatheart of the Nation." The county is located in the great wheat belt of the Southwest and includes both rich soil for farming and grazing and underlying deposits of oil and gas from the Anadarko Basin. The county is also part of the treeless Plains area extending from near the Rocky Mountains through western Kansas, Oklahoma, and northern Texas.

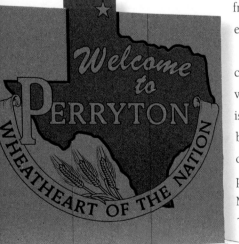

A road trip through Ochiltree County in the fall of the year shows hundreds of combines buzzing steadily along, harvesting the bumper crop of the nation's wheat. Spectacular sunrises and sunsets are enjoyed year-round and are especially beautiful during the wheat harvest, when the sun literally glistens on the amber waves of grain. The writer of "America the Beautiful" must have been traveling through Ochiltree County when she penned the memorable line, "for amber waves of grain."

This page, left: Perryton welcomes visitors to the Wheatheart of the Nation. Photo courtesy of the Perryton Chamber of Commerce

This page, above: Cattle feedlots add much to the agriculture-based economy. Photo courtesy of the Perryton Chamber of Commerce

Opposite page, top: Horses contentedly graze in an Ochiltree County pasture. Photo by Gayle Haygood

Opposite page, bottom: It is often said that nothing separates the Panhandle from the North Pole but a barbed wire fence. Photo courtesy of the Perryton Chamber of Commerce

Oldham  COUNTY

Oldham County, the midpoint of historic Route 66, has a rich history and remains well traveled. The county measures fifty miles by thirty miles and is larger than the state of Rhode Island. The terrain is level prairie land broken by the Canadian River and its tributaries, which form the "breaks." Its history is as vast and diverse as its land.

One of the last areas settled in Texas, the Texas Panhandle was once marked on maps as the "Great American Desert." An early explorer described the Panhandle as a region almost as vast and trackless as the ocean. Pre-Pueblo Indians lived in cliff dwellings along the Canadian River in what would become Oldham County. The county has been home to Kiowa and Comanche Indians, Mexican sheepherders, pioneers, and cattlemen.

When the buffalo trade died with the last slaughter of 1874 and the Comanche were banished to reservations, sheepherder Don Casimero Romero migrated to the area from Mora, New Mexico. Romero came in an ornate coach, with fourteen schooner wagons, one hundred workers, and eight thousand head of sheep to prove that the land was good for grazing.

The native grasses were indeed good for grazing and Oldham County soon became home to some of the largest ranches in the nation. The famous XIT Ranch spread across ten Texas counties from the northern border to south of Lubbock and consisted of 3 million acres. Oldham County was also home to the 221,000-acre LS Ranch and to the Matador Ranch. Today, an average of ninety thousand head of cattle is fed in Oldham County annually.

During the years of the great cattle drives, Tascosa became the hub of the Dodge City cattle trail. First known as *Atascosa*, meaning "boggy creek," for its easy crossing of the Canadian River, Tascosa quickly grew from a one-room blacksmith's shop to a thriving town. In the 1880s, when the total population of the entire Texas Panhandle was only 1,067, Tascosa had a population of 600! When Oldham County

"Paint Rock" is aptly named. Not only does the rock display lovely colors, the rock also is an Indian site where drawings have been found. Photo by William W. Russell

Many arrowheads have been found at this beautiful mesa on the Alamosa Ranch, along with a thirty-room dwelling on top where Indians once lived. Photo by William W. Russell

was formed in 1881, Tascosa became the county seat. The original two-story stone Oldham County Courthouse currently serves as the Julian Bivins Museum on the campus of Boys Ranch.

In 1887, the *Tascosa Pioneer* reported: "Seven saloons. We boom." Tascosa was indeed a booming cow town. Along with lawyer Temple Houston (Sam Houston's son), Billy the Kid and Pat Garrett frequented the town. One story says that Garrett outshot the Kid in a friendly target practice when he drilled a small silver star on a tobacco pouch one night in a dusty adobe saloon.

The small town grew as a trade, trail, and cattle center. Soon, both a cattle trail and mail line developed between Tascosa and Dodge City. Large open-range ranches looked to Tascosa as their hub.

Now famous, Boot Hill Cemetery was a historic part of Old Tascosa and still lies quiet and solemn on a hill overlooking Boys Ranch. Twenty-nine cowboys are buried at Boot Hill and legend has it that the reason it is called Boot Hill is because the cowboys were always buried with their boots on.

Mystery woman Frenchy McCormick, a dance hall girl and the last resident of Tascosa, is a local legend. Only her husband, Mickey, knew her true identity and the secrets of her past. Though she buried Mickey in 1912, Frenchy remained in Tascosa long after it became a ghost town. She vowed never to leave Mickey and Tascosa and remained alone in their adobe home for twenty-seven years.

Shortly after Frenchy left Old Tascosa in 1939, Cal Farley's Boys Ranch was founded on the site, bringing life back to the old town. The old stone Oldham County Courthouse served as home to the first nine boys.

Cal Farley's Boys Ranch, which began with Cal Farley's vision and just nine boys, has grown into a modern community of boys and girls who have found "a shirttail to hang on to" in the midst of a working cattle ranch. Today Boys Ranch serves more than 250 boys and girls a year in a nurturing, Christ-centered, structured community. Children from throughout the United States live in group homes with house parents.

The Boys Ranch Rodeo began in 1944 and six decades later thousands of family, friends, and alumni continue to gather each Labor Day weekend for the annual rodeo and festivities. The boys and girls compete in events from pole bending and barrel racing to bareback bronc and bull riding. The younger children draw the loudest cheers from the crowd as they show off their skills in mutton bustin' and stick-horse barrel racing. In addition to the rodeo, visitors are invited to enjoy great barbecue, cowboy poetry, and living history lessons.

In 1915 (after a five-year battle), citizens voted for the Oldham County seat to be moved from Tascosa to Vega. The population of Tascosa had dwindled and most of the county's residents now lived in Vega, Adrian, and Wildorado. Citizens and merchants had to ride through the breaks and cross the treacherous Canadian River, which at that time had no bridge, in order to conduct official business. One story told is that the county records were stolen from Old Tascosa and that the perpetrators had to swim the Canadian River for the heist!

Oldham County is a tourist Mecca centered on the historic Route 66. Thousands of visitors from all over the world come to get their kicks on Route 66. The small

The Julian Bivins Museum at Boys Ranch. It once housed the Oldham County Courthouse at Tascosa, before the county seat moved to Vega.
Photo by William W. Russell

town of Adrian is actually the midpoint on the famed highway. A large sign welcomes you to Adrian saying, "Welcome . . . Los Angeles 1139 miles . . . Chicago 1139."

Route 66 is America's most historic highway. It was commissioned in 1926 as a link from Chicago to Los Angeles and became known as the "Main Street of America." It was the subject of movies such as *The Grapes of Wrath*, books, television shows, and songs. The famous highway was decommissioned in the 1980s after the Interstate Highway System bypassed many of the small towns, yet Route 66 lives on with a beat of its own.

Vega, the county seat, is home to tourist attractions, many of which front Route 66. Dot's Mini Museum sits where the old section of Route 66 ends. The spunky octogenerian, Dot, shares her collections of a lifetime. The museum is free to visitors and is filled with western artifacts, antiques, and Route 66 memorabilia. The collection is eclectic—everything from blue suede shoes to cattle dehorners. The collection is a tribute to the "Mother Road" and an era that was energizing.

The Magnolia Station, also located in downtown Vega, is a popular tourist stop. The station was built in 1920 and was dubbed the "Magnolia Station on the Ozark

Opposite page top left: The arched entryway into Cal Farley's Boys Ranch is a welcoming sight. Photo courtesy of Cal Farley's Boys Ranch

Opposite page middle left: The Annual Boys Ranch Rodeo is held at the Marshall Cator Arena. Photo courtesy of Cal Farley's Boys Ranch

Opposite page bottom left: Boys Ranchers have fun and learn the ropes at the Annual Boys Ranch Rodeo. Photo courtesy of Cal Farley's Boys Ranch

Opposite page right: The chapel at the Boys Ranch. Photo courtesy of Cal Farley's Boys Ranch.

This page: This structure was built around 1870s by New Mexico sheepherders on the north bank of the Canadian River. This was the first headquarters of the LS Ranch. Photo by William W. Russell

Trail." The "filling station" was unique to that era. The small narrow building not only housed the business but also provided living quarters in a two-room apartment upstairs. First a Magnolia Station, it was also leased to Texaco, Conoco, and Phillips 66 during its years of service. In the 1930s it was named simply the "Hi-Way Service Station."

After closing as a filling station, the building served as a barbershop. The popular Route 66 tourist attraction looks into the past. It tells not only a history of the station, but also illuminates in full color life and travel in the 1920s, 1930s, and 1940s. With gasoline-powered automobiles available to the masses, gas stations sprang up to fill their tanks and keep them on the road. From the migration of the Dust Bowl, through the gas and tire rationing of World War II, to a modern highway with semi-trucks and vehicles of all makes and models, this station tells the story of a nation on the move.

Vega also boasts a fine Heritage and Ranch Museum, featuring outdoor displays of antique farm machinery and equipment. Children enjoy the hands-on opportunity to pretend to drive the tractors and sit on the old horse-drawn plows.

A popular annual county event is the Oldham County Roundup, which is held the second Saturday in August, featuring a free barbecue.

Oldham County has been chosen as the location for several movies, television shows, and music videos and has many interesting facts surrounding it. The total population of Oldham County is 2,185 according to the 2000 Census—almost one square mile for every person. Many more cattle than people live in the county! It is the seventh sunniest area of the United States and is dubbed the Solar Capital of Texas, with more solar heating systems per capita than anywhere else in the state.

A trip through Oldham County is not only a historical visit down memory lane, but also an eye-opening trip to a modern, up-to-date county with a strong economy based on farming and ranching.

This page: Oldham County Sheriff David Medlin sits on the crumbling stone fence where sheepherders placed their herds at night in the Canadian River breaks. Photo by William W. Russell

Opposite page, top: A modern-day cowboy prepares a horse for castration on the Windham Ranch in Oldham County. Photo by William W. Russell

Opposite page, bottom: "Black Gold," in the form of crude oil in tanks, waiting to be trucked to a storage area. Photo by William W. Russell

Parmer

COUNTY

The charming towns of Farwell, Friona, and Bovina are home to the general populous of Parmer County. The county is in the southwest quadrant of the Texas Panhandle and is bordered on the west by New Mexico. It has the distinction of being the only Texas county that was once completely within XIT range. The county has 859 square miles of level plains, which are surfaced by loam, sandy, and clay soils.

The county was founded in 1998 as Parmer Switch on the Pecos and Northern Texas Railway and was named for Martin Parmer, an early settler and Texas Revolution veteran. In 1906 it became the site of a model farm using the Campbell Dry Farming method. The model farm was established by the Capitol Freehold Land and Investment Company of Chicago and raised a lush wheat crop.

In 1907 Parmerton Townsite Company bought two hundred acres of farmland and laid out a town, which was soon designated as the county seat. Later that same year, after a heated election, Farwell was elected as the new county seat. Parmerton's citizens moved to Farwell, taking homes and buildings with them. The railroad switch is the only marker left the Parmerton site today.

As with many Texas counties, Parmer County grew because of the railroad. Parmerton Hill was the highest point on the Santa Fe Railway in Texas. Local folks report that "you can see forever" from the top of Parmerton Hill.

Bovina has the distinction of being the oldest town in the county, as it was where the shipping pens for the XIT Ranch were located. Parmer County lies far south of the geographical center of the famed XIT spread, but, again, holds the distinction of being the only county completely under XIT range.

Border disputes and wars continue today, because the state line between Texas and New Mexico was not correctly surveyed. Farwell, Texas, and Texico, New Mexico, are divided mid-town, and Texas and New Mexico license plates are equal in number in both towns. The state line was settled by a treaty, but the settlers from Iowa, Oklahoma, and North Texas never agreed on the decision. Parmer County,

Bovina has the distinction of being the oldest town in the county, as it was where the shipping pens for the XIT Ranch were located. Photo by James Hurly

Texas residents and Curry County, New Mexico residents keep the battle lines drawn to this day.

The community of Bovina was originally called the Hay Hook Line Camp of the XIT Ranch. The railroad was built through the ranch and a railroad switch was placed so that cowboys could unload cottonseed that had been shipped in as feed. Often the feed was spilled on the tracks, bringing XIT cattle to congregate at the unfenced area. Many times the cattle lay down on the tracks, causing railroad personnel to get off their trains and prod the cattle off the tracks. Because of this, the town was dubbed "Bull Town." County lore suggests that the name was changed because some of the ladies' sensibilities were offended by living in a town called Bull Town. The more refined name of Bovina was chosen and suited the ladies better. The town proudly displays a statue of a bull and is remembered as the largest inland cattle-shipping center in the world.

The cattle business is still the mainstay of Parmer County, with feedlots and dairies dotting the countryside. The feedlot cowboys look much like the XIT cowboys of old and are seen having coffee at the local Dairy Queen in faded jeans, spurs, and chaps. Travelers often get out their cameras to capture photos of real Texas cowboys.

Agriculture is another mainstay of the county's economy, and crops of maize, wheat, and sunflowers are seen in abundance. In the 1960s and 1970s Friona was called the "Maize Capital of the World." Water in the area is not as plentiful today as it was then, causing a reduction in the number of maize and corn crops planted. Dry land wheat farming predominates today.

Friona is the hub of commerce in the county and is the largest town, with a population of more than four thousand. The towns of Farwell and Bovina are home to about fifteen hundred residents each. All of the towns are agricultural centers and boast either a cotton gin or an elevator or both. Lazbuddie is home to two hundred people.

From left to right:

Vintage photo of Friona's Main Street in about 1910. Photo courtesy of Bill and Carol Ellis

Vintage photo of the old Syndicate Hotel. Photo courtesy of Bill and Carol Ellis

The Parmer County Historical Museum is housed in what was originally the First Baptist Church of Friona. It features artifacts of early pioneer life. Photo by Randall Webb

A circa 1910 couple goin' a courtin'. The lady proudly shows off her Easter bonnet. Photo courtesy of Edwina Davenport

In 1907 the Parmerton Townsite Company bought two hundred acres of farmland and platted a town which was soon designated as the county seat. Photo courtesy of Bill and Carol Ellis

Farwell, Texas marker located downtown. Photo by Randall Webb

Beautiful Parmer County architecture with a frame of valued trees. Photo by Randall Webb

Photo conveys the loneliness early settlers must have felt. The vast prairies, lone windmill, and dead cottonwood tree are the stuff western movies are made of. Photo by Darryl Maddox

One of Parmer County's distinguishing marks is the independent spirit of its citizens. They are proud to take care of their own, without federal aid. The Friona Senior Citizens Center serves meals on Monday and Thursdays and is run completely by volunteers and donations. From time to time a group is formed to try to obtain federal funds, but these pioneer spirited folks always refuse. They don't want federal aid, preferring to take care of their community themselves.

Friona was the only school district in Texas that was not forcefully integrated, as they had the distinction of never having had a segregated school. Friona Independent School District is reputed to have had the first school bus system in Texas as early as 1920.

F. W. Reeve, an early mayor and ardent supporter of the schools, helped outfit the bus system. The population of the county follows a similar pattern to Texas as a whole, with more than half of the county identified as Hispanic.

Though they are few in numbers, the residents of Parmer County don't lack for things to do and to share with travelers to their county. The Parmer County Historical Museum is housed in what was originally the First Baptist Church of Friona. Similar to many rural Texas museums, it features artifacts of early pioneer life in the Panhandle. It is open on Saturday mornings by appointment. An art gallery graces the square and adds a cultural note to the county. The "Gallery on the Frio Draw" features artists Bobby Wied, Jim Bob Swafford, and Don Spring.

The annual Maize Days Celebration is held each September in Friona and features a barbecue, a parade, an art show, and school reunions. The county stock shows are also held in Friona each February.

Parmer County has suffered the loss of major industry in recent years, but the resilient pioneer spirit remains and the county is again bustling and beginning to grow.

For a true look at the Old West and real cowboys in action, Parmer County is the place to be.

Potter
COUNTY

To talk about Potter County tourism is to talk about Amarillo, its county seat. Once a flat, barren prairie, Potter County's 902 square miles are now burgeoning with people. It's been said, "If you don't like the weather in the Panhandle, just wait a few hours and it will change"; and "There's nothing between Amarillo and the North Pole but a barbed wire fence!" Actually, the excellent climate is a well-kept secret, and the area enjoys more than three hundred days of sunshine each year. Due to its location on the High Plains, Potter County's elevations range from three thousand to thirty-eight hundred feet above sea level, assuring a lack of humidity on a hot summer day.

Although Amarillo itself is a relatively young city, having been founded in the late 1880s, hunting points and other artifacts that have been scientifically dated indicate that human beings have inhabited the High Plains region for more than ten thousand years.

Francisco Vasquez de Coronado led an expedition across the vast Panhandle grassland in 1541, encountering Native Americans who had never before seen a man of European descent. The arrival of the Spanish explorers would change the lives of the native tribes forever.

As the Texas frontier moved westward in the nineteenth century, colonists established trading relationships with the Plains Indians. However, the Republic of Texas was never successful in establishing territorial control over the region and there were frequent hostile confrontations between the encroaching white settlers and native tribes.

After the Civil War the United States military focused its efforts on controlling and confining the Indian population on the nation's western frontier. By 1875 the Native American population in the Texas Panhandle had been relocated to reservations, making way for an influx of new settlers and huge herds of cattle. The arrival of the regions' first railroad made it possible to transport livestock to eastern

Cadillac Ranch is a much-visited site just off I-40, west of Amarillo. Graffiti encouraged. Photo by Darryl Maddox

markets much more efficiently. In 1888 the town of Amarillo was established next to a huge stockyard where cattle were held before being loaded into railcars.

As the town grew it became the center of activity in the Panhandle, because of its location on established routes leading across the area in every direction. Natural gas was discovered in the area in 1918 and soon dozens of oil and gas companies were exploring the Panhandle Field, the largest known reserve in the world at that time.

With the advent of mechanized agriculture, farmers began breaking sod and cultivating hundreds of thousands of acres of what had been huge fenced tracts of grassland. The search for wealth and work was already attracting many people to Amarillo and by 1930 the city's population swelled to more than forty-three thousand and Amarillo was well established as the region's hub city.

In 1942 the federal government opened two installations that would have long-lasting impacts on Amarillo's future. The military established an airfield at the Amarillo airport, and the Pantex Ordnance Plant, a weapons facility, was built east of the city.

While Amarillo's economy was closely tied to agriculture and the energy industry in the city's early history, it has become more diverse as the city has grown. The arrival of new industry helped shelter Amarillo from the effects of the boom-and-bust cycles endemic to the farming, ranching, and oil and gas businesses. Today Amarillo is home to copper refining, fiberglass production, meatpacking, a helicopter assembly plant, and many more thriving industries and small businesses. It has an extensive medical center complex, boasting both a medical school and a pharmacy school.

Amarillo is well positioned on Interstate 40 and is "on the way to somewhere" for hundreds of thousands of travelers. The fabled Route 66 once traversed through the town and today several blocks of the historic road are a favorite local gathering place and tourist stop. Now called simply "Sixth

Far left: Bell Helicopter assembles the Osprey helicopter in Amarillo, thus Amarillo's nickname, "Rotor City." Photo courtesy of the Amarillo Chamber of Commerce

Below: The Big Texan Steak Ranch is known nationwide as the place where you can get a "Free 72-ounce steak dinner." The catch is, you have to eat it ALL. Photo by Bill Tucker

Right: The famous Route 66 once traversed through the town and is now a favorite tourist place to eat, drink, and antique shop. Photo by Randy Chavez courtesy of the Amarillo Chamber of Commerce

Far right: Wonderland Park is one of Texas' greatest amusement parks and provides summer fun for the Tri-State region. Photo courtesy of the Amarillo Chamber of Commerce

Street," the portion of Old Route 66 passing through Amarillo's San Jacinto Historic District are crowded again with people enjoying the history, the shopping, and the food on the famous route. There are eateries along Sixth Street that are still grilling delicious juicy burgers and crispy fries that early travelers along Route 66 enjoyed in the same location and on the same grill. Antique shops lining both sides of the street offer antiques and artifacts that tell the story of the early Panhandle. Route 66 is a favorite haunt of the local biker populations and motorcycle "Poker Runs" often end at a favorite spot on Sixth.

Undoubtedly the most famous Amarillo restaurant and frequent tourist stop is the Big Texan Steak Ranch, located on the east side of the city on the north side of Interstate 40. "Amarillo, Texas; isn't that the place with the free big steak?" is the question posed when Amarillo folk traveling around the country mention that their hometown is Amarillo. For more than forty years Amarillo and the Big Texan have been the home of the "Free 72-ounce steak dinner" (if, of course, you can eat the whole meal in the time allotted!). Billboard advertisements nationwide have helped put Amarillo and the Big Texan on the map. The family-owned cafe has grown into a massive complex, hosting a large restaurant, a motel, and a horse motel as well.

Wonderland Amusement Park is another favorite area attraction. Located in North Amarillo in the city's Thompson Park on Highway 287, the park hosts thousands of families each season. The fifteen-acre site features more than twenty-five rides designed for all ages, a miniature golf course, food, and arcade games. It is billed as "Texas' Greatest Amusement Park" and although not as big as Six Flags over Texas, it is just as much fun. The complex is well maintained, well lighted, clean, and safe, but most of all fun. Tourists flock to Wonderland Park each season and local families enjoy multiple visits every year.

The Amarillo Zoo is also located in Thompson Park, just southwest of Wonderland Amusement Park. Although the Zoo is small, it is interesting, entertaining, and a place to see many High Plains indigenous animals, termed *Texotic*. Among the animals populating the twenty-acre zoo are grazing bison, a mustang, and the feral horse of the American West. Also in the collection are Texas longhorns, mountain lions, spider monkeys, and a sleek, prowling panther.

Amarillo is home to many fine museums, with collections ranging from art to Indians. One unusual museum is the Kwahadi Kiva Indian Museum and Event Center, located on I-40 East, just west of the Big Texan Steak Ranch. The building resembles an adobe hacienda and displays and fine paintings housed inside depict the cultures of the American Indian people. This unique center is home to the Kwahadi Dancers, a local Boy Scout performing group who present their colorful pageant of song, dance, and stories nationwide. The Kwahadi are the most tenured performing group in Texas and were honored by being given the name *Kwahadi* by the elders of the Comanche Nation.

The Amarillo Museum of Art is one of the hidden gems of the High Plains. It is located on the campus of Amarillo College on a verdant, tree-lined street on the edge of the historic Wolflin residential neighborhood. It is a regional art museum with more than thirteen hundred objects in the fine collection. A special collection contains seventeenth and eighteenth century European paintings, including works by Guardi. The museum hosts fifteen pieces of sculpture, mostly exterior large-scale pieces by contemporary artists and houses a local patron's private collection of early Chinese art and artifacts.

English Field Air and Space Museum is located just east of Amarillo at Amarillo's original airport. This museum celebrates and endeavors to preserve the heritage of aviation of the past and offers the visitor a unique opportunity to experience aerospace. On display is the only Mars Lander on earth. This craft is one of three in existence. The other two are on the surface of Mars. The museum has an extensive

collection of nuclear ordnance, including actual bomb drop units of the Cold War era. English Field is only one of two museums in the world with these artifacts, which are identical in scale to retired thermonuclear weapons.

The Panhandle Art Center is an innovative and practical use of an old, little used shopping center. Sunset Center was built as the first shopping mall in the area in the late 1950s and was a bustling hub of commerce for many years. As the city moved west and newer shopping areas were built, Sunset Center was abandoned. The center is alive and active once again as Panhandle artists use its interesting spaces. The Panhandle Art Center has emerged as the largest artists' co-op in Texas and offers local artisans a place to paint or sculpt and display and sell their wares.

Opposite page: The Globe News Center for the Performing Arts is a magnificent architectural marvel. Photo by Darryl Maddox

This page: The Globe News Center for the Performing Arts features a world-class acoustic interior including a retractable orchestra shell, under a ten-story tower. Photo courtesy of the Amarillo Chamber of Commerce

The Globe News Center for Performing Arts is an architectural marvel, built just across the street from the Amarillo Civic Center. The building changed the face of downtown Amarillo, and the performances inside enrich the area's performing arts. The world-class acoustic interior includes a unique retractable orchestra shell, under a ten-story tower. Not only does the twelve-hundred-seat intimate center house opera, ballet, and the symphony, but cowboy poets, country western groups, and rock groups are also regular performers in the Center.

The Amarillo Civic Center is a state-of-the-art facility located in downtown Amarillo. It is host to a myriad of conventions, meetings, concerts, and special events each year. The 340,000-square-foot complex contains a variety of multipurpose areas, including a ballroom and an auditorium with a fully equipped stage. Large audiences can view a tractor pull, a rodeo, a circus, a rock concert, or an ice hockey game in the center's arena on any given night. The meeting areas house displays from gun shows to antique shows, and are always in use.

Downtown Amarillo is also the final resting spot for the famed Madam Queen Train engine. She sits in her permanent home at Second and Lincoln Streets and is the only (prototype) 2-10-2 "Texas type" locomotive, 5000, especially built for the Plains Division of the Santa Fe Railway. She was built in 1930 and derived her name from an imaginary character on the *Amos 'n' Andy* radio show.

The Polk Street Historic District is a charming two block area located on the edge of downtown Amarillo between Fifteenth and Seventeenth Streets. Visitors enjoy a drive through the past on this historic tour. These houses were built in the early 1900s and are considered the finest stretch of historical residential neighborhoods in the area. Once the most elegant area in the city, the district

includes the Harrington House, Lee Bivins House, J. D. Shuford House, Doheny-Masterson House, Shelton-Houghton House, Galbraith House, Eakle House, and Early House. The Harrington House, former home of local philanthropists Sybil B. and Don D. Harrington, is available for tours by appointment.

Amarillo is the national headquarters of the American Quarter Horse Association and home to the American Quarter Horse Heritage Center and Museum. This unusual museum showcases the history and activities of the American Quarter Horse. Visitors are treated to an exciting exhibit arrangement, informative video productions, and hands-on displays. Exhibits are designed to educate and entertain audiences who know little or nothing about horses, as well as veteran horse owners. From its colonial racing days to its present status as the world's most popular breed, the American Quarter Horse has a colorful history. This history is highlighted at the Heritage Center and Museum. Be sure to stop by the unusual gift shop while you're there.

Art has a free rein in the streets of Amarillo due to a partnership of the American Quarter Horse Association and Center City of Amarillo. More than sixty life-sized sculptures of horses placed throughout the city are sponsored by local businesses and are used as a canvas by local artists, making each one unique. The Quarter Horse is an appropriate icon to symbolize Amarillo, its past and its future.

Amarillo's sprawling Harrington Regional Medical Center's park is the location of two other area tourist attractions. The Don Harrington Discovery Center is a great place for kids to discover the wonders of nature and of science. The center houses more than sixteen thousand square feet of exhibit pace, including a helium area, a weather center, and an extensive marine biology area. Amarillo is known as the "Helium Capital of the World" and the Discovery Center has a collection of artifacts, slides, photographs, posters and documents from the helium plant, which is now

This page: The American Quarter Horse Heritage Center and Museum is an unusual one showcasing the history and modern activities of the American Quarter Horse. Photos courtesy of the American Quarter Horse Association

Opposite page: The historic Bivins Mansion is a part of the Historic District and is the home of the Amarillo Chamber of Commerce. Photo courtesy of the Amarillo Chamber of Commerce

vacant but can still be seen west of the Medical Center. In addition to the exhibit space there is a one-hundred-seat auditorium and a four-thousand-square-foot room of interactive displays. The planetarium is the focal point of the Center and serves to amaze, educate, and create curiosity. The newest addition to the Center is the world's ultimate digital theater system. Amarillo is the fifth installation in the world of the Digistar 3. The space theater takes visitors beyond the stars with educational and entertaining presentations.

Proudly perched in front of the Discovery Center is the Helium Centennial Time Columns Monument. The monument was erected in 1968 to commemorate the hundredth anniversary of the discovery of helium in the spectrum of light from the sun. Amarillo has been the center of activities related to helium since the government purchased the helium-rich Cliffside Gas Field in 1927. The Time Columns Monument consists of four stainless steel time capsules, which are to be opened at specified intervals throughout the years. Each column has a theme represented by the major artifacts sealed within it: man's dependence on natural resources, industry's use of natural resources, science's development of natural resources, and the history of natural resources conservation efforts. The overall height of the monument is approximately fifty-five feet and four spheres within two elliptical rings are suspended from the intersection, representing the molecular structure of helium: two neutrons and two protons orbited by two electrons.

Just next door to the monument one finds the Amarillo Botanical Gardens, to the delight of plant lovers areawide. It offers horticultural education with gardens, an exhibition gallery, lectures, workshops, and hands-on opportunities for school children. A special feature is a fragrance garden planted especially for the blind. This beautiful facility and its surrounding gardens are open to the public.

Perhaps one the most unique sites in the Panhandle is found west and south of the medical

Top: Harrington Regional Medical Center serves people from the Texas and Oklahoma Panhandles, and eastern New Mexico and is the largest and finest medical center between Dallas and Denver. Photo courtesy of the Amarillo Chamber of Commerce

Middle: The Space Theater inside the Don Harrington Discovery Center takes visitors beyond the stars with educational and entertaining presentations. Photo courtesy of the Amarillo Chamber of Commerce

Bottom: Proudly perched in front of the Discovery Center is the Helium Monument erected to commemorate the hundredth anniversary of the discovery of helium. Photo by Darryl Maddox

Potter County is the High Plains center for ropes, rodeos, and any number of equestrian events. Photo courtesy of the Amarillo Chamber of Commerce

center area. It is the often visited, often-written about, often-sung about, Cadillac Ranch. The "ranch" has seen thousands of visitors since it was built in 1974. It is located in a field a short walk from Interstate 40. This unusual site is the brainchild of Stanley Marsh 3, an eccentric millionaire with a love for the arts, particularly environmental art. Marsh owns the dusty wheat field where the ten graffiti-covered Caddies are buried, nose down and fins up, facing west "at the same angle as the Cheops' pyramids." Marsh and the Ant Farm, a San Francisco art collective, assembled used Cadillacs representing the "Golden Age" of American Automobiles (1949 through 1963) to create this unusual Texas attraction. Marsh encourages the many layers of painted graffiti by occasionally repainting the cars. Once, during Breast Cancer Awareness Week, they were painted a bright pink!

Wildcat Bluff Nature Center is another Potter County favorite haunt, north as the crow flies from the Cadillac Ranch. Located on land where cattle once grazed, it is a place to step out of the daily routine and imagine a different time. More than six hundred acres of rolling grasslands are threaded with hiking trails, offering a sense of isolation and tranquility for hikers and nature lovers. Delicate wildflowers, knee-high grasses, and huge cottonwood trees dot the center. Horned lizard, hawk, snakes, and other indigenous critters are routinely spotted along the hiking trails. Wildcat Bluff was named by early cowboys for a den of wildcats that lived under the bluff. It is also the site of a branch of the historic Santa Fe Trail, where wagon ruts are still visible today. It is a place of inspiration, a place to embrace the sprit of the land by exploring the natural magic of the Texas Panhandle.

The Tri-State Fair and Rodeo comes to Potter County the third week of September every year and has been providing fun, entertainment, and good eats since the early 1920s. People from the towns in the tri-state area flock into Amarillo to enjoy the live music, the midway, the exhibits, and, of course, the food. The fair is kicked off by a parade up Polk Street and remains open for the next seven days. The Professional Rodeo Cowboys Association rodeo also takes place during fair week at the Amarillo National Events Center on the fairgrounds.

Potter County is the High Plains center for ropes, rodeos, and any number of equestrian events. Cowboys, cowgirls, and little buckaroos amble into Amarillo and on out to the Events Center to compete or just to watch and enjoy the competitions and the Western ambiance. Team roping, team penning, barrel racing, and bull riding are just some of the events that keep Amarillo on the rodeo map.

The Amarillo Livestock Auction is one of the largest in Texas, selling more than one hundred thousand head of livestock annually. Sale day is every Thursday and is a great day to rub elbows with Texas cattlemen and women and be a part of the true Western experience. The Stockyard Café is a popular eatery at the auction. People come to experience the good "chow," and eat delicious Texas beef. The waitresses have a vernacular all their own and visitors seem to revel in hearing their order

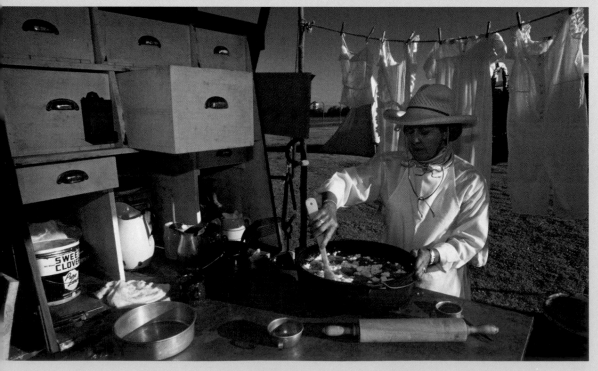

This page: Chuck Wagon cookoffs are popular in the Panhandle with contestants cookin' up some fine vittles. Photo courtesy of the Amarillo Chamber of Commerce

Opposite page: People from area towns flock to Amarillo to enjoy the Tri-State Fair. Photo courtesy of the Tri-State Fair

"hollered" to the cook; "one rib-eye on the hoof and burn another one." Having lunch at the café on a sale day gives a glimpse of the life of a cowman.

Just ten minutes north of Amarillo is a ranch offering the visitor a taste of the real cowboy life style. River Breaks Ranch takes visitors on a ride through the canyon breaks on covered wagons. A stampede storms past as they amble along in the wagon. River Breaks also offers an authentic ranch breakfast or dinner. At the campsite visitors are entertained by horse races and by authentic cowboys roping steers.

Amarillo is a sports Mecca, bringing fans of several sports to the city each season. The Amarillo Dusters play arena football each fall at the Amarillo Civic Center. The Amarillo Gorillas professional hockey team takes to the ice at the center each winter. As hockey season ends, baseball is just beginning. Fans watch the Amarillo Dillas hit those grand slams at the baseball field north of the fairgrounds.

Shopping also brings visitors to Amarillo. Westgate Mall is the largest shopping mall between Denver and Dallas and is conveniently located on I-40 West. Historic Wolflin Village is a beautiful destination shopping experience with its unusual and intimate shops.

Across the street from Wolflin Village sits the Amarillo Little Theater. ALT is a professionally staffed community theater, founded in 1927 and is one of the oldest continuously operating community theaters in the country. It is an important component of the arts community in the Panhandle.

Amarillo remains a transportation hub. The International Airport has the country's longest runway, and one often sees military planes from nearby air bases practicing "touch and go's." The Burlington Northern Railroad and Interstate 40 course through the city. Thousands of semi-trucks and cars travel through Amarillo on the Interstate every day.

Potter County is truly the hub of the Panhandle, its population center, and the destination for medical care, shopping, entertainment, and tourism for the vast High Plains region of Texas.

Randall

C O U N T Y

Randall County and neighboring Potter County are so intertwined that it is difficult even for the county clerks to determine whom to call for jury duty in which county. The sister counties split Amarillo in a zigzag fashion, with the southern part of the town being a part of Randall County. The terrain in Randall County is partly more rugged than Potter and enjoys the benefits of having the majestic Palo Duro Canyon in its midst. Randall County has an area of 922 square miles that extends over an eastward sloping tableland broken by the Prairie Dog Town Fork of the Red River, which flows through Palo Duro Canyon.

Humans inhabited the area more than ten thousand years ago. Evidence of Paleo-Indian cultures and remains of prehistoric animals have been found in both Palo Duro and Cita Canyons. During this period, various nomadic Plains Indian tribes, including the Comanche, Kiowa, and Cheyenne, hunted buffalo in the area and wintered in the canyons.

Francisco Vazquez de Coronado's expedition crossed the area in 1541 and probably camped for a while in Palo Duro Canyon. Fast forward a couple of hundred years and Pedro Vial crossed the county on his way from San Antonio to Santa Fe and then Vial and Santiago Fernandez traversed the canyon as they made their return trip from Santa Fe. While surveying possible routes for a Pacific Railroad, Captain Randolph B. Marcy and Captain George B. McClellan followed the Red River into Palo Duro Canyon before turning north toward the Canadian River.

The massive buffalo slaughter in the 1870s and the Battle of Palo Duro Canyon drove the Plains Indians away from the area. The decisive battle of the Red River War in 1874–1875 was also known as the Buffalo War. This war was the final campaign against the Southern Plains Indians. Colonel Ranald S. Mackenzie, leading the Fourth United States Cavalry, descended a narrow trail into the canyon and attacked the first of five encampments of Comanche, Kiowa, and Cheyenne at dawn. In the panic that ensued, the cavalry captured more than fourteen hundred horses and burned

---

Man has inhabited Palo Duro Canyon for more than twelve thousand years. The Clovis and Folsom people first resided in the canyon and hunted large herds of mammoth and giant bison.
Photo by Darryl Maddox

the Indian's teepees and winter stores. Keeping only the horses he could use, Colonel Mackenzie ordered the remaining eleven hundred shot. Although only four Indians were killed, the coming winter without food or horses meant starvation. The Indians returned on foot to the reservation at Fort Sill, Oklahoma, forever abandoning the life of the hunt. The county was now opened for settlement.

Randall County was separated from the giant Bexar County in 1876 and named for a Confederate general named Horace Randal. History has it that a clerical error doubled the "l" in Randal, thus giving the county its current spelling. The county remained unorganized from 1876 to 1879 and was attached to several neighboring counties.

Charles Goodnight came to the county in 1878, driving sixteen hundred cattle into Palo Duro Canyon. He established his Old Home Ranch as the first JA Ranch headquarters. The following year Leigh R. Dyer built his log ranch headquarters, the oldest surviving building in the northern thirty-six counties of Texas, near the junction of Palo Duro and Tierra Blanca Creeks.

July of 1879 brought formal county organization with an election that named Canyon as the county seat. Ranching reigned supreme as the county's major industry, but open range gave way to fenced pastures in the early 1800s. Registered Hereford cattle were brought into the county in 1883 and the total number of cattle topped

This page: Palo Duro Canyon is called "The Grand Canyon of Texas" and is one of the state's largest parks. The incredibly scenic and beautiful canyon features this shear cliff along the Cita Canyon tributary. Photo by Darryl Maddox

Opposite page: Canyon is the home of West Texas A&M University. Old Main, the administration building is the centerpiece of the campus. Photo by Rik Anderson courtesy of West Texas A&M University

thirty-five thousand by 1900. Farming developed slowly, with oats, sorghum, and alfalfa grown as the first major crops.

The Railroad played a major role in the development of the county. The Pecos and Northern Texas Railway built westward through the county in 1898 and helped bring settlers and a market for crops. The Santa Fe Railway finished the Llano Estacado Railway from Floydada to Canyon, making the first decade of the century a time of dramatic growth for the new county.

The 1920s brought the next surge of new growth. The number of farms more than doubled and cattle ranching continued to be of primary importance. Sheep ranching was introduced into the county by 1900, reaching an all-time high of more than thirteen thousand head in 1930. Croplands harvested also more than doubled during the 1920s, with a large percent of the cultivated acres devoted entirely to wheat growth.

The Great Depression of the 1930s hit the county hard. Falling prices, drought, and the devastating dust storms of 1935–1937 were contributing factors. The work programs, such as the Civilian Conservation Corps, and increased use of irrigation helped the county weather the Dirty Thirties.

Randall County became progressively more urban as Amarillo moved south from Potter County into north central Randall County. By the 2000 census, more than 104,000 people lived and worked in Randall County. Agriculture continues to play a crucial role with cattle and wheat the dominating forces in the rural economy. Education, tourism, and manufacturing are also essential elements to the commerce of the county.

Canyon bills itself as the "Gateway to Palo Duro Canyon." It is a bustling community located off Interstate 27, just ten minutes south of Amarillo. Nestled in the middle of the Texas Panhandle, Canyon claims a rich history based in cattle and ranching, and a heritage rooted in the pioneer spirit of the West. The city has many parks, a municipal swimming pool, excellent golf courses and tennis courts, and utilizes the International Airport in nearby Amarillo.

Festivals, fairs, fireworks, and parades are enjoyed throughout the year and shopping is also on the top of the "to do" list while in Canyon. Texas art, antiques, crafts, and apparel, can all be found in Canyon. The picturesque setting of the historic Town Square adds to the shopping experience.

Canyon is the home of West Texas A&M University. The school was chartered in 1897 as West Texas State Normal College and remains the only four-year University in the Panhandle. Old Main, the building housing the school's only classrooms, laboratory, library, and offices, burned in 1914; but the college carried on its work in temporary quarters until a new building was completed. The name was changed to West Texas State Teachers College in 1923 and in 1931 it was the first institution of higher learning in West Texas to offer graduate training. In 1942 a building was given to the college in Amarillo and the college began to offer adult education classes in Amarillo. Annual enrollment for the college averaged one thousand and in 1949 it became West Texas State College. Another name change occurred in 1992 when the Board of Regents authorized the name change to West Texas A&M University when it became a part of the Texas A&M system. Today WTAMU is a comprehensive university, offering more than sixty undergraduate-degree programs and forty graduate-degree programs. The student enrollment is approximately seven thousand.

Old Main was rebuilt after the fire and had a $5 million renovation in the late 1980s. A new Fine Arts Complex will open soon. Athletic events, fraternities, sororities, and a myriad of other activities enhance campus life. West Texas A&M certainly contributes to Canyon's healthy economy.

The Panhandle-Plains Historical Museum sits on southwest corner of the tree-lined campus of West Texas A&M University campus and holds the distinction of being the largest history museum in Texas. With a vast collection of more than three million artifacts, the Panhandle-Plains Historical Museum lives up to Texas' reputation of being the biggest and best! Visitors to this fine museum have an opportunity to relive the stories of courage and hardship, victory and defeat of the pioneer days. Or they can leap back twenty million years, getting close up and personal with a prehistoric rhinoceros (Aphelops) or a life-size meat-eating Allosaurus in the extensive paleontology collection.

Another route follows the board sidewalks of Pioneer Village, an authentic turn-of-the-century settlement complete with all the buildings and furnishings of a thriving town of that era.

The museum hosts an immense transportation exhibit, from trails to rails, foot power to horsepower, and automobiles to aviation.

The oil boom of the 1920s and 1930s is majestically displayed in the petroleum wing's two floors of exhibits. The exhibit depicts how the Plains' scrubby ranchlands were transformed into oil-soaked "patches" bristling with drilling rigs.

This page left: These beaded moccasins are Western Sioux, circa 1900, on display at the Panhandle-Plains Historical Museum. Photo courtesy of the Panhandle-Plains Historical Museum

This page above: The museum has Kiowa Chief Big Tree's headdress, circa 1900, on display. Photo courtesy of the Panhandle-Plains Historical Museum

Opposite page left: The Panhandle Plains Historical Museum. Photo by Rik Anderson courtesy of West Texas A&M University

Opposite page right: The mountain lion exhibit is enjoyed by this father and son. Photo courtesy of the Panhandle-Plains Historical Museum

Opposite page bottom: The carriage exhibit shows a family preparing for a trip. Photo courtesy of the Panhandle-Plains Historical Museum

The museum also has an exhaustive collection in its art galleries, featuring works of nationally recognized southwestern artists, including Georgia O'Keeffe, who once taught at West Texas A&M University.

The Panhandle-Plains Historical Museum has become the repository of some of the finest American Indian art in the entire country. One gallery highlights Native American baskets, as well as beautiful examples of beadwork, pottery, textiles, silver and turquoise jewelry, paintings, and sculpture. The museum also houses the largest collection of historical Texas flags in the country. This museum is a "must see" when in the Texas Panhandle. It is really five museums in one, with sections dedicated to petroleum, western heritage, paleontology, and art.

Palo Duro Canyon is the most important tourist attraction in the entire twenty-six counties of the Texas Panhandle. It is appropriately called "The Grand Canyon of Texas" and is one of the state's largest parks, with more than eighteen thousand acres. The scenic canyon has incredible spires and pinnacles that have been carved over the centuries by a branch of the Red River. Walls plunge almost a thousand feet to the canyon floor, exposing brilliant multicolored strata.

Man has inhabited Palo Duro Canyon for more than twelve thousand years. The Clovis and Folsom people first resided in the canyon and hunted large herds of mammoth and giant bison. Later on, other Indian cultures utilized the canyon's abundant resources.

Early Spanish explorers are believed to have discovered the area and dubbed the canyon *Palo Duro*, which is Spanish for "hard wood," in reference to the abundant mesquite and juniper trees. An American did not officially discover the canyon until 1852 when Captain Marcy ventured into the area while searching for the headwaters of the Red River.

The canyon was privately owned until 1933 when it was given to the state for use as a state park. From 1933 until 1937 the Civilian Conservation Corps (CCC) sent six companies of young men and military veterans to Palo Duro Canyon to develop road access to the canyon floor and build the visitor center, cabins, shelters, and the park headquarters. Palo Duro Canyon State Park officially opened on July 4, 1934.

A gift of Cañoncita Ranch was added to the state park in the early 2000s and the Texas Parks

This page top: Palo Duro Canyon's eroding slope of Triassic Age clays and Permian Age sands and silts. Photo by Darryl Maddox

This page bottom: Children throughout the years have been fascinated by Devil's Slide. It is one of the most popular locations in Palo Duro Canyon. Photo by Darryl Maddox

Opposite page: The last light of sunset illuminates an anvil cloud over Palo Duro Canyon. Photo by Stephen C. Pardy

and Wildlife Department purchased more than two thousand acres adjacent to the park along the southern boundary, adding more scenic acreage.

Park activities include camping, horseback riding, hiking, nature study, bird watching, mountain biking, and scenic drives. The Old West Stables, located inside the canyon, offer guided tours to Timber Creek Canyon and the famous Lighthouse formation. The native stone visitor center is located on the canyon rim and houses historical displays and a well-stocked gift shop.

Due to its diverse habitats, Palo Duro Canyon contains many species of wildlife, including the rare Texas Horned Lizard and Palo Duro Mouse. Other species include the wild turkey, white tail and mule deer, aoudad (Barbary) sheep, coyote, cottontail rabbit, roadrunner, and western diamondback rattlesnake. On the canyon rim, longhorn steers, which are a part of the official Texas State Longhorn Herd, may be viewed from the main road.

The canyon is approximately one hundred miles long, twenty miles wide, and eight hundred feet deep. Extending from Canyon to Silverton, Palo Duro Canyon was formed primarily by water erosion, which began to carve the canyon many years ago. The slopes of the canyon reveal the colorful natural history of the area. Dating back 250 million years, the oldest layers of rock, Cloud Chief Gypsum, can only be seen in a few areas in the canyon. The next oldest and most prominent layer of rock is the Quartermaster Formation with its distinctive red claystone/sandstone and white layers of gypsum.

A beautiful amphitheater rests in the canyon and is the backdrop for the sensational outdoor drama *TEXAS*. A six-hundred-foot-tall cliff serves as the kaleidoscopic backdrop for the play. Whether in tears of passion or determination, the settlers of the Texas Panhandle had one thing in common: a romance with the West. Their pioneering spirit and willingness to risk anything to achieve everything kept their hopes alive. The romance extended beyond the land and into each other's hearts. This Paul Green outdoor drama is beautifully written and performed and is in its thirty-ninth (2006) season. The dramatic story, dynamic musical score, realistic effects, and state-of-the-art lighting and sound effects make this an outdoor drama extraordinaire. The famous lightening scene and the fireworks finale raise goose bumps on even the most stoic audience members. A Texas barbecue dinner is available before every performance. The drama begins in early June and ends in mid-August.

The Elkins Ranch is a popular haunt at the entrance to the Canyon. Visitors can enjoy an authentic chuck wagon supper prepared by real cowboys; or if getting up early one morning and enjoying a Panhandle sunrise is more appealing, a chuck

This page: Magnificant wall of Permain Age shales along the Lighthouse Trail in Palo Duro Canyon. Photo by Darryl Maddox

Opposite page, left: The Lighthouse at Palo Duro Canyon is probably the most recognizable landmark of the Canyon. Photo by Norbert Schlegel

Opposite page, right: Fall colors along the Lighthouse Trail make Palo Duro Canyon even more breathtaking. Photo by Norbert Schlegel

wagon breakfast is also available. Jeep tours, Native American heritage tours, and live western entertainment round out the Elkins' offerings.

Just west of Canyon is the German Catholic community of Umbarger. The population remains stable at about 325 and the town's claim to fame is the famous Umbarger Sausage Festival, held at St. Mary's Parish Hall each November.

Near Umbarger is Buffalo Lake National Wildlife Refuge, one of the major waterfowl refuges on the Central Flyway. The 7,677-acre haven is a winter home for a million ducks and eighty thousand geese. Once known as Tierra Blanca Water Conservation Project, the lake now holds very little water, but the refuge continues to draw visitors on its interpretive walking trail and 4.5-mile auto interpretive trail. Activities include picnicking, sightseeing, birding, nature study, and photography. Campsites with tables and grills are available. The refuge headquarters sits three miles south of Umbarger on FM (Farm-to-Market Road) 168.

In north Randall County, located in Amarillo, is the Texas Panhandle War Memorial. A relative newcomer to Amarillo, the memorial sits proudly at I-27 and Georgia as a tribute to area veterans, living and deceased, who served the United States in a branch of the armed forces. This peaceful memorial boasts a large red granite archway, a lovely circular garden, and granite tablets featuring the names of those who died or are missing in action. A carillon tower plays music on the hour.

Randall County is buzzing with activity and the construction of new homes, churches, and businesses. The fifteen-mile drive between Amarillo and Canyon offers a view of a bustling microcosm of commerce. The sister towns of Amarillo and Canyon have almost grown together, making them the metroplex of the Panhandle.

Roberts COUNTY

Welcome to woolly mammoth country! Imagine walking the Plains over twelve thousand years ago. No people, no cars, no life as we know it today. Now imagine walking among enormous prehistoric woolly mammoths contentedly munching on moss, lichens, and shrubs.

Bones of the woolly mammoth were discovered in Roberts County in 1933 when a local farmer's plow unearthed some large chalky bones—much too large for a cow or a buffalo. The unusual find caused a full archeological excavation and the Miami Site was found to contain a plethora of bones later identified as those of the large fossil elephant, known as the woolly mammoth. This large pachyderm is known to have become extinct more than ten thousand years ago. Previously, archeologists had thought that the earliest North American human inhabitant, the American Indian, had roamed this area about two thousand years ago. Many of the man-made artifacts found in association with the archeological excavation of the Miami Site were significant, indicating that man lived and walked these Plains along with the giant woolly mammoth. The Miami Site was among the first to clearly show contemporary existence of man and mammoth. Many of these bones and artifacts are in storage at a research center in Austin, Texas, but many are also available for viewing at the Roberts County Museum.

Fast forward a few thousand years to 1876 when this same land, formerly inhabited by prehistoric man and animal, emerged as a settlement in the Wild West. Invention of the windmill and barbed wire made the Panhandle more inviting to early settlers. The railroad, too, caused people and commerce to converge on the once desolate plain.

Roberts County as we know it today, nine hundred square miles with a population of 850, was carved out of the original Bexar County land in 1876 and received county status in 1889. A county seat war ensued between the ranchers at Parnell, a community to the north of Miami, and the citizens of Miami. The Parnell ranchers opposed organizing in Miami because of probable higher taxes on their

Reflections on a pond. Photo by Loralee Cooley

large grassland holdings. The visionary Miami folks, who came with the railroad, wanted control of the county and its taxes to build a modern Roberts County Courthouse and to promote settlement. Temple Houston, son of Sam Houston, who represented Miami, waited until a commissioner in the Mobeetie Courthouse was sick to present the petition for an election to the Commissioners' Court. The slightly tainted vote was two to one, and round one went to Miami.

Miami won the subsequent election by a landslide, but Parnell appealed and won. The district judge threw out the 1889 election after taking a good hard look at the ballots cast by "Mr. Buzzy" and his twenty-one sons. A search for the prolific Mr. Buzzy revealed that neither he nor his progeny were any longer in the county. Round two to Parnell.

A three-year battle of lawsuits, countersuits, stolen county records, kidnapped officials, a cameo appearance by the Texas Rangers, and general mayhem followed. Miami land promoters worked hard to get more settlers, which in turn meant more voters. In 1892, the second election favored Miami, and the county seat was secure. The scars lasted for years, however, and a large quantity of Roberts County taxes were never collected.

In 1887, Miami was the nearest railhead to Fort Elliott and handled more than one million pounds a month in freight for the fort. Growth was rapid until the 1926 oil boom in Borger and Pampa when many people moved to take advantage of better

jobs and higher wages. In two short years Miami went from a population of fifteen hundred to half that number. Large land holdings and the growing neighboring towns dampened the development of Miami. However, the small town along the tree-lined banks of Red Deer Creek has found its niche as a county seat, local trade center and a great place to rear a family or retire.

Today's Miami (pronounced "my am i") is a beautiful little town with a population of a few more than eight hundred. This tiny burg, nestled in the southeast part of the Panhandle, is a getaway Mecca for those busy souls wanting to escape the hustle and bustle of city life. "There is not a lot to do in Roberts County. That is why you would want to come to Roberts County," said a local economic development official. Vacationers enjoy watching the birds, the flowers blowing in the wind, and generally taking a good deep breath of fresh air away from the television, the traffic, and the telephone. The big cities offer plenty of rollercoasters, traffic jams, and night life. A vacation in Roberts County offers peace, quiet, and breathtaking natural beauty all around.

Opposite page: The excellent Roberts County Museum is housed in the original Santa Fe Depot. Photo by Randall Webb

This page, left: The annual cow calling contest originated in 1949. Cow callers compete by hollering for the cows to come home. Photo by Leslie D. Espinosa

This page, middle and right: The Roberts County Courthouse, built in 1913, sits on a grassy slope overlooking Miami, the only municipality in the county. Photos by Randall Webb

Miami's economy is centered on farming and ranching, but the town has plenty to offer visitors. Miami boasts an exceptional city swimming pool and beautifully maintained park in addition to the Roberts County Museum. The museum is a source of education for the young and a nostalgic look at the past for the old. The museum's site itself has a history. It was the location for the local blacksmith shop behind the garage and "filling station." The original Santa Fe Railway Depot was purchased in 1878 and moved to the museum's current location. The depot is an artifact itself, having served the people of Miami since 1888. The museum boasts prehistoric artifacts and fossil bones, in addition to interesting vignettes of early pioneer life. Indian artifacts, arrowheads, primitive tools, and a large collection of early ranch brands are popular exhibits. Wildlife dioramas entertain visitors and a trip to the half-dugout completes the fascinating journey through this exceptional museum. With a glimpse inside the dugout, one realizes how little our forefathers had to help them exist in this barren, windswept section of Texas.

Miami's annual "Cow Calling" event is held the first weekend in June and has garnered national attention. The weekend begins with the much-anticipated "follies" on Friday night and continues on Saturday with the free Fireman's Barbecue, awards, all-school reunions, art shows, and the cow calling contest. A country western dance ends the festivities. When Maggie Gill, a local celebrity, was featured calling cows on Johnny Carson's *Tonight Show,* the annual Miami celebration garnered national attention.

The fall of the year features the annual Fall Foliage Tour, which begins in nearby Canadian and continues through Roberts County. Thousands of tourists enjoy the scenic drive to immerse themselves in the spectacular colors of fall.

Miami's town slogan sums it all up: "Life is good in Miami, Texas." Come see for yourself.

Sherman

COUNTY

Sherman County is a hunter's paradise. Stratford, the county seat of Sherman County, is best known for its incredible pheasant hunting and is proud to be called "The Pheasant Capital of Texas." Each December hunters arrive clad in fluorescent orange caps and vests. They tote an arsenal big enough to protect a small village and begin the serious yet fun month of pheasant hunting. The town of Stratford and the surrounding area's farmers and ranchers embrace the pheasant season. Ring Neck Pheasants are vibrantly beautiful birds, each weighing about three pounds. A permit to hunt is required and only cocks may be shot. The state-imposed limit is usually two to three cocks per day.

Another, more unusual kind of hunt, has recently come to the forefront in Stratford. This hunt knows no season and generally requires no fee. Hunters from all over the country are coming to Sherman County to hunt the furry little rodent called the prairie dog. These hunters, too, come field-equipped with small tripods and rebored .22 rifles with scopes. They lie on their bellies, guns stabilized with the tripod, enjoy the hunt, and also help rid the area of an unwanted pest. Prairie dogs don't like cultivated land and generally gravitate toward areas of native grasses. Prairie dog hunting began in about 1992 and has grown into a popular sport. Area children have been shooting the prairie dogs for years and now the sport has moved into mainstream hunting. The local landowners appreciate the hunters' ridding of the pests from their land and the hunters just have fun. One area landowner said, "It's sort of like an arcade game where you try to 'whack a mole.' The cleanup is easy . . . just walk away after the hunt and let the coyotes and buzzards take care of the cleanup."

The breeding of Morgan horses and longhorn cattle is a new addition to Sherman County's economy. The Greentree Ranch relocated its headquarters from Longmont, Colorado, to Stratford to breed and train its champions. The family-owned business dates back to the early 1960s. Greentree has been successful in its goal to produce a combination of bloodlines, environment, care, and training and has

"I can see for miles and miles and miles," penned in a song and so true in the vast open prairie of the Texas Panhandle. Photo by Ann Wells

Photo credits clockwise from bottom left:
Stratford schools began in 1901 and are a center of
community focus. The Stratford Elks are extremely
competitive in sports, band, and academics. Photos by
Gaynelle Riffe

When the song "America the Beautiful" talks about amber
waves of grain, it must be talking about the beautiful Texas
Panhandle. Photo by Becky Asher

First baby buffalo born in Sherman County in more than a
century Photo by Gaynelle Riffe

Stratford hosts carriage entourages in late September. The
drivers wind through town and end up at the County Barn.
Photos by Gaynelle Riffe

Two mighty combines are cutting wheat
during the fall wheat harvest. Photo by
Becky Asher

never wavered from that goal. The ranch family works hard to preserve and enhance the true Morgans, with as little deviation as possible. Horses bred at Greentree range from beloved family horses to world champion show horses and from trail horses to dressage winners.

Stratford and Texhoma are the primary communities in Sherman County. Wide-open spaces with separate and distinct seasons make Sherman County an attractive place to live and work. The county's irrigated farming of wheat, corn, and grain sorghum, along with confined animal feeding operations, makes this "Tip Top" area a great place to call home.

Stratford is home to more than twenty-five residences dating back to 1900–1910. These beautiful historic homes dot the town, creating an aura of days gone by. Additionally, the county's Sherman County Museum is located in the old Railroad Depot downtown. Four cemeteries dating from the 1890s are of special interest, because the county provides an index of the graves.

Animal feeding is essential to the Sherman County economy, both cattle feeding and contained pork operations. Good grass, water, and grain provide a habitat for abundant wildlife. Petroleum is also an important economic staple in the county.

Stratford is called the "Tip Top Town in Texas" and is located in western Sherman County at the crossroads of two major highways, US 287 and US 54. Railroads also intersect at Stratford. The Union Pacific and the Burlington Northern Santa Fe haul the nation's goods through Stratford.

As is the case of most towns in the Texas Panhandle, the railroad played a large part in Stratford's development. Aaron Norton purchased one hundred sections of land from the railroads and settled the area around 1885. The town was named by Norton's hired manager after Stratford, Virginia, the boyhood home of General Robert E. Lee. Colton, originally from Kentucky, had been a devotee of General Lee and was happy to impart that same name to the new town site in Texas. In 1900 the site that Colton's group platted became a shipping point and post office on the

Left: Welcome sign.

Middle: Harvested pheasants.

Right: Pheasant on the prairie.

Chicago, Rock Island and Gulf Railway. Coldwater was the original county seat, but an election in 1901 resulted in Stratford's replacing it as the county seat. There was a dispute over Stratford's right to be the county seat of government, even though there had been an election. The Texas Rangers were called in to settle the matter and Stratford finally emerged as the new county seat.

In 1901, George M. Kerr began a new county newspaper, the *Stratford Star,* which continues to report the news today. Homesteaders and small business people were attracted to the area by advertisements placed by the Standard Land Company, a Rock Island immigration agency based in Kansas City, which established a ranch office in Stratford.

By 1910 Stratford boasted three churches, a school, two banks, and a population of more than 600. The town continued to grow, and by the late 1920s, when the Panhandle and Santa Fe Railway arrived it was a thriving little town. The Dirty Thirties hit Stratford hard and although the Dust Bowl posed a threat to the local economy, programs of the Agricultural Adjustment Administration and the Work Projects Administration, and later the introduction of irrigation wells, enabled Stratford to continue to grow as the center of Panhandle agriculture. In the 1980s several large feedlots and feed production plants came to the area, as well as a steel fabrication plant, a tannery, a bank, an airport, seven churches, enlarged public schools, and an exhibit and livestock show barn. Stratford was incorporated in 1940, when it reported a population of 877, and today is home to almost 2,000 hardy folk.

Texhoma is Stratford's sister city in Sherman County and is located just twenty miles northeast of Stratford. The residents affectionately say that Texhoma is so big that it takes two states to hold them! Livestock and agriculture bolster the Texhoma economy. Texhoma is unique in its bicameral city council form of government (one for each state). This quiet Texas/Oklahoma community of 350 citizens has three city parks and a municipal airport.

Although Sherman County is most noted for its incredible hunting of pheasant, pronghorn antelope, dove, and prairie dog, its open spaces, sunsets, sunrises, and clear blue skies are unforgettable.

Left: On his last visit home before shipping out to France in 1917, this Sherman County young man shows some Panhandle patriotism. Photo courtesy of Nita L. Dyslin

Right: Sherman County brother and sister show off their homemade Sunday best in the midst of the family's dryland maize crop in the early fall of 1916. Photo courtesy of Nita L. Dyslin

Swisher COUNTY

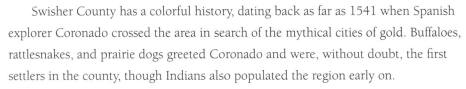

Swisher County has a colorful history, dating back as far as 1541 when Spanish explorer Coronado crossed the area in search of the mythical cities of gold. Buffaloes, rattlesnakes, and prairie dogs greeted Coronado and were, without doubt, the first settlers in the county, though Indians also populated the region early on.

The area that is now Swisher County was the home of Apachean cultures that were displaced by the more warlike Comanche by around 1700. The Comanche dominated the High Plains until they were defeated by the United States Army in the Red River War of 1874. During the war, Army troops crisscrossed Swisher County in pursuit of the Indians, but no real fighting occurred in the county. The decisive battle took place in Palo Duro Canyon in 1874 and severely crippled the Comanche. By the mid-1870s hunters were exterminating the massive herds of buffalo.

The Texas legislature soon created Swisher County from lands that had previously been a part of the Young and Bexar Districts and by 1890 four hardy souls were living in the area. As the buffalo were exterminated, cattle ranching came to the county. Colonel Charles Goodnight and John Adair expanded their JA Ranch operations into Swisher County and built the first log cabin in the area, used as a line camp and headquarters for this new Tule Ranch. The ranch occupied the entire eastern part of the county and the cabin was located near a spring and a watering hole about twelve miles east of the present town of Tulia. The ranch cowboys were instrumental in organizing the county, and settlers often found seasonal employment on the ranch.

By the late 1880s the scattered settlers of the county realized that they needed an organized local government and a petition for organization was circulated in June 1890. The tiny settlement of Tulia was chosen as the county seat. Swisher County remained a wholly ranching community until the early 1900s. As late as 1890 there were slightly more than 525 improved acres on the county's seventeen ranches, with only one hundred settlers living and working in the county. By the late 1890s a few settlers began farming operations.

Young "Okie" steer represents the present-day herds in Swisher County. Photo by Randall Webb

It was about this time that drought and a plague of grasshoppers swept the Plains and many settlers were forced to leave their holdings. These events halted the growth of the area until a state representative from Plainview introduced changes in a land bill called the Four Section Act. This bill reclassified the land as "grazing" at the price of one dollar an acre instead of the previous two dollars an acre, causing a resurgence of interest in the area. Soon after the Four Section Act, most of the public lands were utilized by homesteaders.

Quanah, Texas, was the nearest railroad point at that time and lumber to build dugouts and homes was hauled from there. W. G. Conner and his family filed on the section of railroad land on which Tulia was built. They built a dugout, which was the first home in Tulia. He gave the land for the school, the courthouse, and the city park, which still bears his name. It is also reported that he gave each person who would vote for Tulia as the county seat a twenty-five-foot city lot.

The area had good underground water at shallow depths, and windmills increased the farmers' opportunities to become successful. The county's ranching and farming operations continued to grow and by 1906 a Santa Fe Railway branch line reached Swisher County. When the track was completed to Lubbock in 1910, Tulia and Swisher County were on a major north-south rail line. Railroad construction also led to the establishment of two new Swisher County towns, Kress and Happy. The new railroad was a boost to economic development in the county, tying the area to national markets and easing immigration.

As agriculture increased in importance to the county's economy, wheat became a major crop. Wheat became even more desirable during World War I, as it was vital to feeding the world. This, together with a price of up to $3.50 a bushel and the introduction of tractors and combines, caused hundreds of acres of land to be put into cultivation immediately following the war and during the early 1920s. The drought that followed, along with poor farming practices, brought on the Dust Bowl of the 1930s. The stock market crash and depressed prices brought about the Great Depression. During this time of great hardship, many farmers were driven from their homes and the population of the county declined.

Though there had been a few attempts at irrigation as early as 1912, it was not until 1936 that it began to be a force in the economy. By the early 1940s, with the higher prices for farm products due to World War II, rubber-tired tractors and cotton strippers, more farms put down irrigation wells and a new era of prosperity was initiated. During these years, many believed that the supply of irrigation water was inexhaustible and tail water flowed freely down the borrow ditches into lakes or creeks. Between 1910 and 1920 Tulia became known as the City of Windmills, because of the proliferation of windmills in the vicinity.

Wheat, grain sorghum, cotton, and soybeans became staple crops and livestock continued to be important. Four-lane highways crossed the state and county. Level plains, once barren, were now laden with color. Summertime brought acres of golden wheat and fall saw mile after mile of brown and gold milo, fields of dazzling white cotton, and hundreds of black- or white-faced cattle grazing on green wheat fields. Imposing ranch-style brick homes arose where the pine lean-tos or half-dugouts once stood.

The 1950s and 1960s saw the introduction of the feedlot, utilizing local grain and hay to fatten cattle. It soon became apparent that the water supply was not limitless and water conservation became more and more important. Tail water pits were dug and studies were underway for the best utilization of water in the county.

By the 1990s Swisher County had developed an agricultural economy based on a mix of cotton, wheat, grain sorghum, corn, oats, barley, and soybean production, balanced by hogs, sheep, and cattle, primarily fed in feedlots.

Opposite page: Between 1910 and 1920 Tulia became known as the City of Windmills because of the proliferation of windmills in the vicinity. Photo courtesy of the Tulia Chamber of Commerce

This page: Entrance to Swisher County Feedlot. Photo courtesy of the Texas Cattle Feeders Association

Today Swisher County is home to almost eighty-five hundred folks and has remained a center for farming and agribusiness activities. The population of the county is concentrated primarily in its small towns, which include Tulia, the county seat, Happy, Kress, Claytonville, and Vigo Park. The remainder of the population lives on surrounding farms and ranches.

The county seat of Tulia is home to the largest percentage of the population, and it is here that most visitors are attracted. The Swisher County Museum, housed in downtown Tulia, is a natural stop for visitors to the county. Paintings are on display, along with pioneer relics and a log cabin that was originally a line camp for the JA ranch. The J. O. Bass Collection is a "must-see" in this museum. Mr. Bass was a Tulia blacksmith and was noted for his finely crafted bridle bits and spurs. His blacksmith shop is recreated in the museum and Bass bits and spurs sell today on eBay for thousands of dollars.

The Kenneth Wyatt Gallery draws visitors from across the globe. Dr. Kenneth Wyatt is an internationally prominent artist, sculptor, and writer, with studios in Tulia; Red River, New Mexico; and Naples, Florida. Tulia is the central base for his business and he is often in the studio working at his easel. Visitors are free to watch and talk to him as he works. His daughter, Jill, is a fine water-colorist and his wife, Velda, a sculptor of some renown. The Wyatts also design and manufacture jewelry, using mostly semi-precious stones and high-quality pewter.

Another favorite haunt of locals and visitors is the famous El Camino Restaurant. This Mexican restaurant has been owned and operated by the same family for more than forty years and features consistently delicious Tex-Mex cuisine. Locals laugh when they say, "When we tell people that we're from Tulia, Texas, they invariably say, 'Oh, that's where that wonderful Mexican restaurant is'!"

An original Ozark Trail marker still stands on the Town Square as a reminder that Tulia was a major stop on that historic route. Tulia has a nine-hole municipal golf course, an airport, a Girl Scout camp, and a privately funded park. The stage at Tule Creek Park is the site each summer of a bluegrass festival, held the second weekend in July. The town's original Royal Theater has been restored and hosts live shows, melodramas, and the National Champion Fiddlers' Contest.

The annual picnic and rodeo is held in mid-July and includes an old settlers' reunion. It is one of the longest-lived continuing celebrations in the Panhandle and is called simply "The Picnic." This celebration features a parade, a rodeo, a carnival, art exhibits, and barbecue. The 2006 Picnic was the 116th year for this annual event.

Tulia's neighboring town to the north, Happy, gives motorists a smile as they approach it from either direction on Interstate 27 and see the sign "Happy, The town without a frown."

An original Ozark Trail marker still stands on the Town Square as a reminder that Tulia was a major stop on that historic route. Photo courtesy of the Tulia Chamber of Commerce

OZARK

TRAILS

'EAST

SILVERTON -32
QUITAQUE -53
TURKEY -65
ESTELLINE -100
MEMPHIS -107
WELLINGTON -132
HOLLIS OKLA -145
OKLA CITY -325
CHANDLER -378
STROUD -392
TULSA -450
MONTE NE ARK -531
JOPLIN MO -588
SPRINGFIELD -669
KANSAS CITY -728
ST LOUIS -928
PITTSBURG KAN -545

T
H
S

HORNETS

TULIA   TULIA
SWISHER CO.   SWISHER CO.

Wheeler COUNTY

Wheeler County, 914 square miles of rolling prairies and rough river breaks, is on the eastern edge of the Texas Panhandle, very close to the Oklahoma border. The fertile red sandy loam and black clay soils produce bountiful native grasses, wheat, cotton, sorghum, and alfalfa. The creeks and other watered areas in the county produce abundant mesquite, cottonwood, chinaberry, willow, hackberry, black walnut, and oak trees.

What is now called Wheeler County was the early home of a Plains Apache culture. This way of life was followed by a modern Apache society, which was displaced by the Kiowa and Comanche around 1700. The Kiowa and Comanche dominated the Panhandle until their defeat in the Red River War in 1874 began their move to reservations in Indian Territory in 1875 and 1876. Prior to 1874, this rolling plain in the eastern part of the Texas Panhandle was entirely unoccupied by white man.

In 1875 buffalo hunters began moving into the northwestern part of what is now Wheeler County and established a rudimentary outpost called "Sweet Town" or "Sweetwater." Sweetwater, now often referred to as "Hide Town" because of the buffalo hides that covered the picket framed buildings, grew under the protection of Fort Elliott, a post established by the United States Army in June of 1875 to help deter Indians escaping from Indian Territory. The Fort remained active and contributed to the economic development of the county until October of 1890.

The population grew around Hide Town and Fort Elliott and in 1876 the Texas legislature established Wheeler County. After the buffalo were annihilated, ranchers began moving into the area to use the lush, free grass for grazing livestock and many became wealthy cowmen. Others began to settle in the area and nearby Sweetwater quickly became a bustling frontier town. Soon the necessary 150 qualified voters to warrant organizing the county (white men over twenty-one years of age) were living in the area.

Texas sign sits proudly on the Texas/Oklahoma border on I-40/Route 66. Photo by Norbert Schlegel

In 1879 Wheeler County gained the distinction of becoming the first organized county in the Texas Panhandle. On applying for a post office in Sweetwater, the town name was refused by the postal department because the town of Sweetwater in Nolan County was already granted a post office. A county commissioner was married to an Indian woman and in her language the word for sweet water was *Mobeetie*. The town was renamed and Mobeetie became the first county seat of Wheeler County. For two years Wheeler County had jurisdiction over the other twenty-six counties of the Texas Panhandle. Any business of the courts took place in Mobeetie.

Mobeetie reached its peak population in 1885 and was host to a large business district, many hotels, boarding houses, and restaurants. However, the growth of Mobeetie halted suddenly in 1888, when two railroads were built in the Panhandle and both of them missed Mobeetie. In 1903 the Fort Worth and Denver Railway came across the southern edge of the county and the town of Shamrock blossomed. It is now the largest town in Wheeler County.

Because the United States realized there was no further need to protect the settlers from marauding Indians, the Army abandoned Fort Elliott and with it went the bulk of Mobeetie's trade. A tornado further diminished the town's population. The wood-framed Wheeler County Court House was moved from Mobeetie to Wheeler in 1907 after a county-wide election moved the county seat to the new town of Wheeler.

Mobeetie today is a delightful little burg of just more than one hundred residents. The town is reminiscent of the Old West, with the former jailhouse a focal point. The jail is now a museum and an interesting place for Wild West aficionados to tour. Mobeetie is known as the "Mother City of the Panhandle" as it is the oldest town in the twenty-six county region. The original flagpole for Fort Elliott now stands at the Mobeetie Jail Museum. The poles were cut from the cedar breaks on the Canadian River, just northeast of the fort. The poles were each about fifty feet long and were joined together to make the flagpole.

The original gallows, created to carry out the death penalty, remains within the walls of the jail. The jailhouse museum also hosts artifacts and information concerning the Red River Wars, Price's Battlefield, buffalo soldiers, women of the West, Fort Elliott, and buffalo hunters.

Left: A Kiowa ribbon dancer steps proudly to the drum in a beautiful feathered costume. Photo by Leo Shuler

Right: Calvary reenactors march across the parade ground of Fort Elliott. Photo by Leo Shuler

Mobeetie saw its fair share of the Wild West. It was here that a gunfight over a card game and a dancehall beauty named Mollie left a young Bat Masterson with a limp he would carry the rest of his life. Henry O. Flipper was stationed at Fort Elliott in 1879 and has the distinction of being West Point's first African-American graduate and the first African-American officer in the United States. The legendary captain of the Texas Rangers, "Cap" Arrington, enforced law and order as sheriff of Wheeler County, at the time the judicial district for the twenty-six counties.

Natives and visitors relive those Wild West days each summer when the Mobeetie Music Festival is in full swing. Held the fourth weekend in July, this music festival attracts fans from all across the United States. Labor Day brings the Old Settlers Reunion to Mobeetie. Toe-tapping entertainment and a free pit barbecue lunch bring hundreds of people and their lawn chairs to the special day.

Wheeler was centrally located and was deemed a good choice as the new county seat. The city's early economy was based on agriculture and cattle ranching. As the word spread farther south into Texas about the "Garden of Eden" in Wheeler County, the population began to increase.

Wheeler evolved purposefully, as a small group of men envisioned more than one hundred years ago. Because Wheeler was planned and built to be the county seat, it has always been economically stable. Wheeler is a picturesque town and is remote, but not isolated. Several highways connecting Amarillo and Oklahoma City intersect at the town's only stoplight.

WHEELER COUNTY COURTHOUSE AND JAIL

The statuesque Wheeler County Court House stands proudly in the center of town. Its 1927 architecture is reminiscent of a more respectful time. Wheeler is a city with an abundance of American pride. The city holds an old-fashioned Fourth of July celebration each year, filled with fun, food, and entertainment.

An old rock schoolhouse, dating back to 1886, still stands today. It is located on the Britt Ranch and is a constant reminder to all who see it of the desire of the pioneer ancestors to educate themselves and their families.

Visitors enjoy Wheeler and the Great Texas Wildlife Trail. The infinite vistas, rolling prairies, and amazing Plains sunsets add to an unforgettable wildlife trek. The limitless horizons reveal North America's great ocean of grass. A short fifteen-minute drive north of Wheeler puts you square in the middle of the most scenic, well-managed, and exciting wildlife habitat remaining in this part of Texas. In addition to the rare lesser prairie chicken, Wheeler County's vast ranchlands and wetlands are home to a variety of wildlife from prairie dog to soaring hawk.

Shamrock, the largest town in the county, is on Interstate-40 (formerly Route 66). This bustling community is host to hundreds of semi-trucks, RVs, and tourists

Top: Wheeler was centrally located in the county and was deemed a good choice as the new county seat. Circa 1900. Photo courtesy of Norbert Schlegel

Bottom: The statuesque Wheeler County Court House stands proudly in the center of town. Its 1927 architecture is reminiscent of a more respectful time. Photo by Norbert Schlegel

each day and provides more than four hundred hotel rooms for sleepy travelers.

Although the name *Shamrock* suggests an Irish heritage, the town was primarily settled by German immigrants. The name was first suggested by an Irish immigrant sheep rancher, for good luck and courage, when he applied in 1890 to open a post office at his dugout home. Shamrocks do, however, grow wild in the county and perhaps that same sheepherder saw them growing outside his dugout.

Agriculture and oil support the economy of Shamrock. It is not unusual to see cattle grazing happily in the same pasture where an oil jack is pumping.

The Reynolds Hotel, built in 1928, has become the Pioneer West Museum and definitely deserves a look. It was open as a hotel for fifty years and hosted many a weary traveler. The museum has twenty-five rooms full of historical pioneer settler and Indian artifacts. It also houses the Prairie to the Moon Space Room, with articles on loan from NASA's Houston Space Center.

A tourist focal point in Shamrock is the beautifully restored U-Drop Inn Cafe. This unique building was erected of brick and green glazed tile in 1936 and served the area as a service station and café for many years. It is said that in its day the U-Drop Inn Cafe was the swankiest of swank eating places and the most up-to-date edifice of its kind on U.S. Highway 66 between Oklahoma City and Amarillo. The U-Drop-Inn, where "Delicious Food Courteously Served" became the standard, was a welcoming sight to the many buses and cars full of highway travelers that stopped at the diner.

The diner, restored in 2002, houses the Shamrock Chamber of Commerce and Economic Development Offices. It still stands as a welcoming beacon to all who see it and provides a glimpse into a gentler time. The Tower Station and U-Drop-Inn is one of the most interesting and eye-catching points of interest along Historic Route 66.

Shamrock's world-famous Saint Patrick's Day Celebration is held annually on the weekend nearest March seventeenth. A lively parade, which stretches for blocks, begins the celebration. As many as ten thousand people attend this annual Irish celebration. Other festivities include a rodeo, craft show, car show, poker run, chili cook off, carnival, bake off, dance, and the much-anticipated crowning of "Miss Irish Rose." The Saint Patrick's Day Celebration was the brainchild of a Shamrock bandmaster who envisioned the town of Shamrock capitalizing on its Irish name and producing an annual one-day celebration to draw thousands of visitors to the city. The first festival kicked off in 1939 and the extravaganza continues each March.

Bill Mack, the legendary XM cowboy, continues to tout his childhood home of Shamrock, Texas, on his popular radio show. He's often heard saying . . . "Shamrock, towering over Texas." The statement is true, as the Shamrock Water Tower is the tallest municipal water tower in the great state of Texas.

Though today it is home to more than five thousand people, Wheeler County is a well-kept secret. Its beauty, history, and "much to do about everything" deserve a second look.

Top left: *Idyllic scene at the North Fork of the Red River with the old US 83 Bridge in the background.* Photo by Norbert Schlegel

Top right: *The Tower Station and U-Drop Inn Cafe was built in 1936 on historic Route 66. It was beautifully restored in 2004.* Photo by Norbert Schlegel

Bottom left: *The windmill and barbed wire were very important in the settlement of the West.* Photo by Norbert Schlegel

Bottom right: *The Shamrock water tower is the tallest municipal water tower in Texas.* Photo by Norbert Schlegel

Index

About
THE AUTHOR

MARIWYN McPHERSON WEBB

A lifelong resident of the Texas Panhandle, Mariwyn was born in Clarendon and grew up in Amarillo. As the daughter of an elementary school teacher, she began writing as a child and never stopped. Her mother laughs as she says that *imagination* was one of her first words. She is the author of a children's book: *Rodney, The Texas Ghost* and is a contributing writer for *Accent West Magazine* in Amarillo.

Mariwyn is a seasoned veteran with more than twenty-five years as an advertising, public relations, and marketing executive, winning hundreds of awards on the regional and national and international levels. She founded a multimillion-dollar advertising agency and managed the day-to-day operations as well as serving as the agency's creative director. As a creative strategist, she became known nationally for her keen instincts and flair for innovation.

She is active in community affairs and is a political activist. She served as a delegate to the White House Commission on Small Business and was featured in an article on women entrepreneurs in *Texas Business Magazine*. She is passionate about literacy and has spent the last several years working on the national level to help reduce illiteracy in America.

She spends her spare time traveling with her husband, Randy, and enjoying her family. As an only child, she is extremely close to her parents and her two grown sons. She plans to continue writing. The great-American novel is rolling around in her head and is next on the drawing board.